Smart Guide™

to

Estate
Planning

About Smart Guides™

Welcome to Smart Guides. Each Smart Guide is created as a written conversation with a learned friend; a skilled and knowledgeable author guides you through the basics of the subject, selecting the most important points and skipping over anything that's not essential. Along the way, you'll also find smart inside tips and strategies that distinguish this from other books on the topic.

Within each chapter you'll find a number of recurring features to help you find your way through the information and put it to work for you. Here are the user-friendly elements you'll encounter and what they mean:

The Keys
Each chapter opens by highlighting in overview style the most important concepts in the pages that follow.

Smart Money
Here's where you will learn opinions and recommendations from experts and professionals in the field.

Street Smarts
This feature presents smart ways in which people have dealt with related issues and shares their secrets for success.

Smart Sources
Each of these sidebars points the way to more and authoritative information on the topic, from organizations, government agencies, corporations, publications, web sites, and more.

Smart Definition
Terminology and key concepts essential to your mastering the subject matter are clearly explained in this feature.

F.Y.I.
Related facts, statistics, and quick points of interest are noted here.

What Matters, What Doesn't
Part of learning something new involves distinguishing the most relevant information from conventional wisdom or myth. This feature helps focus your attention on what really matters.

The Bottom Line
The conclusion to each chapter, here is where the lessons learned in each section are summarized so you can revisit the most essential information of the text.

One of the main objectives of the *Smart Guide to Estate Planning* is not only to better inform you how to get your affairs in order before you go, but how to plan ahead to make the most of what you have now.

Smart Guide™
to
Estate Planning

Laura Spinale

CADER BOOKS

John Wiley & Sons, Inc.

New York • Chichester • Weinheim • Brisbane • Singapore • Toronto

Smart Guide™ is a trademark of John Wiley & Sons, Inc.

Copyright © 1999 by Cader Company Inc. All rights reserved
Published by John Wiley & Sons, Inc.
Published simultaneously in Canada

This publication is designed to provide accurate and authoritative information in regard to the subject matter covered. It is
sold with the understanding that the publisher is not engaged in
rendering professional services. If professional advice or other
expert assistance is required, the services of a competent professional person should be sought.

Library of Congress Cataloging-in-Publication Data:
Spinale, Laura.
Smart guide to estate planning / Laura Spinale.
p.   cm.   — (Smart guide series)
Includes index.
ISBN 0-471-35360-4 (pbk.: alk. paper)
1. Estate planning—United States Popular works. I. Title.
II. Series: Smart guides.
KF750.Z9S68   1999
346.7305'2—dc21   99-32350

Printed in the United States of America

10 9 8 7 6 5 4 3 2 1

This is for the whole
Jeoffrey's/Winberries/Trivial Pursuit/Java & Cream crowd.
What can I say? You saw me through.

But mostly this is for my dad:
I remember where the box is now.

Acknowledgments

With grateful acknowledgment for the insights and expertise of all the estate-planning professionals, lawyers, accountants, and tax planners who have shed their share of light on estate planning for this book. And thanks to those nice people at Lark, who really know how to pull up the rear.

Contents

Introduction

You're going to die.

Probably not today, probably not tomorrow, perhaps not even for another decade or so. But sooner or later, each one of us must, as Shakespeare put it, "shuffle off this mortal coil."

There's nothing you can do about it.

The goods you've accumulated over the course of your life—your cash, your house, your stocks and bonds, your great-grandmother's diamond engagement ring—will survive you.

Deciding how you want these assets dispersed is called "estate planning."

And you can do quite a lot about planning your estate.

The process is sometimes tricky. Those lucky enough to bequeath large legacies may wonder how to give as much of their assets as possible to their loved ones, and as little as possible to the tax man. Those of more modest means will worry about how their debts will be paid after their death.

On whichever end of the socioeconomic spectrum you sit, the *Smart Guide to Estate Planning* can help.

Read this book and you'll learn to:

- **Chart the Course.** With this you'll calculate your net worth, and decide which of your assets you wish to leave to which loved ones. To some family members, goods of sentimental value may prove as important as a cash legacy. Frank discussions with your heirs can diffuse potential family feuds surrounding the dispersal of your estate.

Some legacies are so complex that you may need to assemble an estate-planning team to make sure all contingencies are covered.

- **Keep the Tax Man at Bay.** In the year 2006, legacies totaling $1 million or less won't be subject to federal taxes. The bad news is that $1 million isn't as much as it used to be. You can avoid federal taxes by starting to draw down your estate now. Give gifts of up to $10,000 to any one you like, tax free, in any calendar year. Married couples can double that amount. The unlimited marital deduction allows you to give any amount to your spouse, tax free, each year.

- **Write a Will.** Wills are the backbone of most estate plans. They are the only document through which you can legally name guardians for your minor children. They also serve as a perfectly fine primary estate-planning tools for people just starting their career and for those who simply don't want to be bothered with the complexities of setting up trusts. Beware, though: wills are subject to the long, and often costly, probate process—and your heirs generally can't touch your assets until legitimacy of the will is established. Other estate-planning tools allow for a smoother transfer of assets.

- **Establish Trusts.** Trusts are legal systems through which you or your loved ones reap benefits from, and sometimes even control, without technically owning them. They can help reduce your estate-tax levy, and, since they bypass probate, they provide for a smooth transfer of assets. Though more expensive to draw up than a simple will, and more confusing to understand, they often serve as the most sound estate-planning tools.

- **Choose Your Life-Insurance Plan.** Mention the words "life-insurance options" and most people's eyes start to glaze over. Still, life insurance is a necessary purchase for anyone on whom others depend for financial support. Term life insurance pays your heirs predetermined benefits upon your death. Cash-value plans fulfill the same role, and also offer a savings component. While the kids are still small, it's usually a good idea to insure the family homemaker. Retirees with an income of at least $30,000 a year and other substantial assets, may want to consider buying private nursing-home insurance.

- **How to Handle Family Concerns.** Let's face it—you must appoint personal guardians to care for your children should you die before they reach adulthood. You can set up trusts for minor children, and even for adult "kids" who may be incapable of handling an outright cash legacy. Finally, if you want your family business to survive your death, you must set up a succession plan.

- **Plan for a Change.** No one really likes to think about the end of his life, but spending a few hours planning for that inevitability can ensure that your wishes are followed at a time when you are no longer able to speak for yourself. Learn how to write up a living will and give a trusted confidante your durable power of attorney for health care. Consider planning your own funeral and writing your own obituary. Last, take the time to write an ethical will—it will give your loved ones a concrete reminder of the precepts by which you tried to live your life.

By now you may be thinking, "Well, this all sounds nice, but a little on the complicated side.

I'm just going to scribble a note listing who gets what. I'll leave it in my files. That should take care of everything."

Think again. This type of "no plan" estate plan does nothing to protect your assets, or your loved ones.

Read on and you'll learn why you absolutely need to plan your estate and how to get started.

CHAPTER 1

·······················

You've Got an Estate

THE KEYS

• Your estate comprises your cash and cash equivalents (stocks, bonds, and so on), your real estate, and your personal property.

• Wills, trusts, and other estate-planning tools transfer your assets into the hands of your loved ones after your death.

• If you die intestate, your state government will determine which of your loved ones receive your assets.

• You can minimize the tax levy on your estate by giving away some of your assets now.

• To begin planning your estate, you'll need to gather deeds, bank account records, stock records, and other pertinent information and documents.

You've got an estate. You may board your thoroughbreds in your family's ancestral country manor, or stash your baseball-card collection in your $400-per-month apartment. For spending money, you may either dip into the multimillion-dollar trust fund established for you by your grandfather, the robberbaron, or you may literally dip into your change jar. On whatever end of the socioeconomic rainbow you sit, you have finances and property that will be disbursed after your death.

Let's face it, though—if you're reading this book, you probably sit somewhere in the middle. You have a nice house, a couple of kids, and a career or business you're reasonably happy with.

And, if you're like most Americans, you've avoided planning your estate. You've avoided it for two perfectly natural reasons. First, you're afraid that you don't have as much money as you go around thinking you do. As embarrassingly ostrich-like as it may seem, many people would rather not know the full truth of their financial situation.

The second reason? You don't want to die—don't even want to think about it.

Therefore, you've chosen to disburse your assets through the hastily-scribbled-note-on-the-kitchen-table method.

The note reads something like this:

Dear Folks:

Susie is making me write this letter. We're heading off to Vegas tomorrow, and she's deathly afraid of flying.

So, if we, both perfectly healthy 35-year-olds, should go down in a fiery crash, this is what you need to know.

Our son, Blake, is staying at his uncle Bobby's house for the week we're away. If we should die, though, we want our best friend, Jennifer Stevens, of 123 Maple Street, to raise him.

Jennifer will need cash to bring up the Blake. To get it, you should sell the house (there's still $100,000 owing, but the sale should net a few grand). There's also about $20,000 in receivables due to my company, Tom's Building, Inc. Jennifer should get that money, too. And don't forget the bank accounts (another $30 grand or so) and our $500,000 life insurance policy. Blake is named as beneficiary if Susie and I die simultaneously.

That's about it.

> *Take Care,*
> *Tom*

FAA officials will attribute the crash of United World Airways, Flight 111, Anytown, U.S.A. to Las, Vegas, Nevada, to "mechanical failure." As Tom and Susie wing their way to the afterlife, he will look at her and say, "I'm so glad you had me write that note, Honey. Now we know that our child will be provided for."

Think again.

This is what will really happen.

Uncle Bobby will hear of the crash on the six o'clock news. He will calm Blake. Then, using his spare key, he will enter Tom's house and read the note. Uncle Bobby is savvy enough to know that he can't just assume guardianship of Blake, so he calls his county social services agency. The social workers descend on his home and decide whether Uncle Bobby is capable of at least temporarily caring for Tom and Susie's child—now a ward of the state—or not. If "not," Blake will be placed in foster care until a fitting home is decided by the local family court. Bobby, also realizing that Tom and Susie have assets to be disbursed, but having no clue where to find them (Tom didn't note in his

F.Y.I.

When the word "estate" was first used to mean "everything owned," only the landed gentry—masters of great mansions and vast tracts of land—wrote legal documents to ensure their legacies went to the right people.

F.Y.I.

Eighty percent of Americans are intestate (don't have a will).

SMART SOURCES

The American Association of Retired Persons publishes a host of literature on estate planning. Many of these publications also offer specific, up-to-date information on estate laws and taxes nationwide. Contact the organization at:

1909 K Street, NW
Washington, D.C.
  20049
(202) 434-2277

letter which bank he and Susie used, or from which company they bought their life insurance), will hire a lawyer. The lawyer, familiar with state intestacy laws, will attempt to inventory the couple's assets. Breaking into Tom's Building offices, he'll find Tom's invoice list. Unfortunately, accounts receivable only total $5,000, not the $20,000 Tom noted in his letter. (Tom took all the information about his primary, $15,000 account, with him. He thought he could get some work done on the plane.)

As to other assets? The lawyer will monitor Tom and Susie's mailbox, waiting for a monthly bank statement—which he gets soon enough. Now he at least knows in which institution the couple kept their savings. The life-insurance premium bill may take up to another year—meaning that it takes this long for the lawyer to figure out which company actually issued Tom and Susie's policy. Only then can he apply for the payout that will benefit their son.

The cash won't all go to Blake. The lawyer, of course, will need to be paid for his time. If Tom and Susie's estate exceeds current federal credit, part of it may go to the IRS. Finally, state intestacy laws vary from venue to venue. Tom and Susie may have lived in a jurisdiction that mandates giving siblings a percentage of their legacy. So Tom's estranged sister, Helen, is able to lay claim against the estate.

Then there's Jennifer Stevens—the woman Tom and Susie wanted to raise Blake. She's willing, and able, to do so. The only problem is, Bobby won't relinquish his claim to the boy. In lieu of a will, custody courts usually mandate that care of minor children go to the deceased's next of kin. In this case, Uncle Bobby.

Uncle Bobby is a man filled with wonder and light. Tom and Susie were thrilled that he has a close relationship with their son. The only problem? He's a little unmotivated. He's 43 years old, lives in a smallish rented loft, and is still hoping to make it as an artist some day. So, when Blake hits 16, he'll sit down with his uncle and say, "Bobby, you know what? I've gotten just as much as I can out of this whole school thing. I think it's time to get out, now." To which Bobby replies, "Hey, go find yourself, kid."

Fast forward to Blake, at 38, in charge of French fries at Big Burger Bonanza.

Scared yet?

You should be. To put it plainly, if you don't plan your estate properly, courts will determine the fate of your assets for you.

Conversely, a sound estate plan will effect an orderly transfer of your assets to your family. The plan will ensure that your family is taken care of, minimize the specter of your heirs fighting over their inheritance, and keep your wealth from disappearing into taxes and lawyers' fees.

What if you're wondering about the estate benefits to paying for your children's education? What if you doubt that your spouse could cope with the details of your estate? What if you and your spouse die simultaneously? Who would manage your estate for your underage children? And at what age should your children start receiving your assets? You can address all these issues through your estate plan.

Need more?

Without planning, your survivors are likely to be unprepared for estate tax, meaning that your property and real estate may have to be quickly liquidated, making your survivors sellers in a buyers'

SMART SOURCES

The American Bar Association publishes an introductory booklet called *Planning for Life and Death*. To obtain it, contact the organization at:

750 North Lake Shore
  Drive
Chicago, IL 60611-
  4497
(312) 988-5000

market. So much the worse if, for instance, real estate prices are down and treasured holdings disappear for a fraction of their actual worth.

If you become disabled to the point of being unable to handle your finances, and haven't planned your estate, someone beyond your choosing will be appointed to handle this chore. And if your spouse ends up in a nursing home, without estate planning all of your assets could end up paying those bills.

You've already started getting smart about estates by learning what can happen to your family if you don't plan. Now it's time to review your current financial circumstances, and learn how to gather the information you'll need to get started on your estate blueprint.

What's the Point of Estate Planning?

In the simplest sense, estate planning is the process of assessing your current circumstances to prepare for your future. At the same time, you'll start to take control of your finances by taking a good hard look at what you have now, and weighing that against what you'd like to own one day. Planning your estate, you'll become more aware of your finances than ever before.

A Hard-Won Lesson in Estate Planning

Financial consultant Peter Cross, of Financial Associates in Marblehead, Massachusetts, recently heard a true horror story. His neighbor's grandmother in California learned the hard way what happens when an estate isn't planned.

"This woman, Jeanette, never had to work outside of the home. Her husband, Carl, was well paid as a skilled laborer and he worshipped the ground she walked on. He more or less carried her around on a pedestal. She never had to pay a bill, or even think about when it was going to get paid."

Then, at 62, the husband died suddenly of a heart attack. The family assumed that he had provided for her well by leaving a great deal of money in the bank. And he had. The only problem, though: he hadn't left a will, or other estate plan.

The chaos was considerable. In a panic, Jeanette called lawyers, who only confused her, prompting her to call even more lawyers. After court costs and lawyers' fees, almost everything was gone. Jeanette never remarried and she lived to be 94. She spent the rest of her life on Social Security.

"My neighbor learned that you need to take the time to plan your estate," says Cross. "Don't procrastinate. And don't the mistake of thinking the court has your interests in mind when they're forced to do it for you. It won't come out the way you want. My neighbor saw what happened to her grandmother, and it wasn't a pretty sight."

Keeping Track of Your Current Investments

You've probably already started investing for the long haul. You want to retire someday, and you're going to need that nest egg. You probably also want to send your kids to college, and maybe afford your grandkids the same opportunity. Estate

F.Y.I.

If you wish to reduce the size of your estate you can make annual tax-exempt gifts of $10,000 per recipient. If you're married you can double it.

planning is partially dependent on your current worth, and partially dependent on the investments you will make in the future. Keep your current investment strategy in mind as you begin planning your estate, and determine what holes you need to plug.

Life insurance, for example, will adequately provide for your family in case of sudden death, and if you don't yet have it, strongly consider buying some. If, on the other hand, you're lucky enough to live just about forever, living trusts and powers of attorney may be necessary.

As you look at your financial situation, you may realize that you have accumulated an estate that exceeds the federal estate-tax credit limit set by the federal government (you'll learn all about this in chapter 3). So take some steps to leave your loved ones as much as possible and the IRS as little as possible. Beginning to give away your money now—to your friends, family, and charitable organizations—will not only make you feel good, but can help bypass costly levies on your eventual estate.

Planning Is an Ongoing Process

You never stop planning your estate. Your blueprint isn't some sort of monolithic, dusty decree that will one day be read in solemn tones in a paneled room. It is a vital program—an ongoing exercise of annual review. Your life will change. Tax and estate laws will change. Your estate plan must change with them.

As you begin organizing, it is essential that you

view the estate-planning system that you'll undertake as something you'll return to again and again for the rest of your life.

Your Estate-Planning Team

While this book provides you with a thorough introduction to estate planning, you'll almost certainly need various professional advisors.

You most likely already have an accountant, and perhaps a lawyer as well. You're going to need an insurance representative and possibly a financial adviser. The role of each will be discussed in the next chapter.

This might sound like an awfully large (and expensive) team, but remember the ounce of prevention. If you don't pay now, your survivors could end up paying much more later.

The Documents You'll Need

Before you begin planning your estate, you'll need to gather all the documents that delineate what you have to give away. Ultimately, you will add copies of your will, trust agreements, your life insurance plans, and your gift and donation schedules and gift tax returns to this filing system.

The original documents for your will: trusts; insurance policies; stock certificates; deeds; birth, marriage, and death certificates should be kept in a fireproof lock box or in a safe-deposit box at your bank.

SMART DEFINITION

Probate

From the Latin meaning "to prove," as in proving honesty, probate is an expensive and time-consuming court review of a will for approval. The purpose is estate evaluation and the establishment of ownership; the result is fees and taxes. One of the biggest reasons for estate planning is avoiding probate.

F.Y.I.

You can't avoid probate by not having a will. If you die without a will, one will be written for you. In probate court. A judge will make your decisions for you as a surrogate (which is why probate is sometimes called "surrogate court").

For now, you must include these crucial documents in your estate files:

• Federal and state tax returns for the last seven years

• Personal financial statement

• Business financial statement (variously, your balance sheet, profit/loss statement, cash-flow statement, operating statement, and/or income statement)

• Two most recent pay stubs

• Your employer's summary of employee benefits

• IRA and Keogh statements

• Profit-sharing and pension statements

• Mutual-fund account statements

• Brokerage confirmations

• Health- and disability-insurance policies

• Deeds to real estate and appraisals

• Mortgages and notes

• Amortization (payment) schedules

• Property- and casualty-insurance policies

Organize these documents in a secure—but not secret—place. You must be able to get at your estate files when you need them. Your heirs must also be able to lay their hands on this material when you're no longer around to tell them where you've hidden it.

Get a box of file folders, a portfolio case, or accordion files large enough to hold them. If you have a filing cabinet, clear out a drawer. This will be where you keep your vital documents relating to your estate. Organize it in such a fashion that it is easy for you to reference and will allow easy access for your survivors and anyone else who might be involved in settling your estate. Write out a file guide or "table of contents" and update it with each file change.

Make sure that your heirs know where you keep your "estate files." Write anyone likely to be involved in your estate—your spouse, children, executor, anyone relevant—a "leave behind note," telling them where they can find this information. Your note should include:

• Description of what you have stored

• Where you have stored it

• A list of professionals with whom you have worked (lawyers, brokerage firms, bankers, and others) and their telephone numbers

• Your executor's name and phone number

• Your trustees' names and phone numbers

(Don't worry if any of these terms are foreign to you—you'll learn all about trustees and executors in the following chapters.)

SMART DEFINITION

Will

A legal document expressing your wishes for the distribution of your estate after you die, including, if necessary, whom you want to take care of your children in your absence.

Beneficiary

Strictly speaking, a person you choose to give to when you make a will, while an "heir" is someone who will receive the assets of your estate.

Executor

A person you name in your will to make sure that your wishes, as expressed in that document, are adhered to. The executor "executes," or carries out, your plan.

Lock Box versus Safe-Deposit Box

Some people are just lock-box-in-the-den-closet types and some are safe-deposit-at-the-bank types. And you probably already know which of these sorts of people you are. What you and all these other people have in common, though, is the need to have a safe, disaster-proof place to keep important documents, including your will, birth certificate, marriage certificate, stock certificate, and the like.

The lock box is a just right if you want your stuff immediately at hand and under your careful watch. This is an understandable perspective. Be aware, though, of this basic fact: this box, which lives in your house, stands the same chance of disappearing in the event of a burglary as, say, your computer or jewelry or television. And then all of your important, irreplaceable, original documents are gone. A sobering thought.

The safe-deposit box, then, has the appeal of being safer from the whims of the sticky fingered, though it's not so easily accessed as the lock box in the closet. Sure, it only takes a quick trip to the bank to deposit or remove items from the box, but there's a little more to it than that.

In the event of a person's death, the law requires a very specific way of handling the entry into a safe-deposit box by family members or lawyers or anyone else who seeks access to the items inside. If the box was rented in the names of a husband and wife, the surviving spouse is generally granted unrestricted access to the box. Or if the next of kin needs to search the box for a will or burial instructions or whatever, the bank allows access upon presentation of a death certificate. Otherwise, the bank is obliged to bar access to the deceased's safe-deposit box until the IRS takes its requisite peek inside.

So, finally, the lock box is just different from the safe-deposit box, not better or worse. And you pick which one you want to use based on your own requirements and comfort level. But do pick one, because you don't want your important original documents stored hither and yon, or in danger of being stolen or damaged, or unavailable to those who need them when it counts.

Your Plan to Plan: Just Do It!

Make it your goal to understand how all the pieces of the estate-planning pie save money, time, and trouble for you and your heirs. This book is designed to help you make informed decisions. There are books on "do it yourself" wills and others on "do it yourself" trusts. This book isn't one of them. But you can do most of the groundwork yourself. You can walk into the office of any member of your estate-planning team armed with knowledge and turn those billable hours into billable minutes. With this information, you can save your team members' time, and, therefore, save yourself some money.

This book will get you started and comfortable.

We'll start, in the next chapter, by determining exactly what you own, and to whom you want to leave it.

WHAT MATTERS, WHAT DOESN'T

What Matters
• Getting started now. Even the simplest estates will take time to arrange. (And you could always die tomorrow . . .)

• Planning with the assets you have now. No matter the amount, your net worth is what you've worked to accumulate, and you have the right to say who gets it after your death.

What Doesn't
• Using an estate plan to get even. The point of estate planning is to avoid trouble, not create it.

• Waiting until you have more money. The time is now; don't let opportunities pass you by till "your ship comes in."

• Worrying about dying. The grim reaper comes for us all. No use fretting about it.

Sample "Leave Behind Note"

Dear Kids,

As you know, your mom and I have, over the last few years, been actively updating our estate plan. No, this isn't a letter to rehash who gets what and why (I think we've settled all that during our recent conversations). Rather, we want you to know where you can find all the information you'll need in the event of our deaths.

We have stored all our estate-planning documents in the top drawer of the gray filing cabinet in my home office. In the very first file of that drawer, you'll find a long letter detailing exactly what that drawer contains. (A copy of our will, our life insurance policies, bank account numbers, brokerage information, etc.)

As you know, we've named you as coexecutors of our will. You will probably need to contact the following people after our deaths:

1.   Our estate lawyer: Mark Sutcliffe, Smith & Sutcliffe, New York, New York, (212) 555-1234.

2.   Our life-insurance representative: John Smith, Caring Hands Insurance Company, Westchester, New York (914) 555-7890.

3.   Our stockbroker: Henry Fields, Fields Investment, Inc., New York, New York (212) 555-8721.

4.   Our funeral home: Marks & Noble Funeral Home in Sommerville, New Jersey (908) 555-7274.

(Remember, we have bought a full, prepaid funeral plan, covering everything from the viewing room to our plots and caskets.)

That's about it, Susie and Mark. As a family, we've joked about both of your organizational abilities, or lack thereof, but please, please find a safe place to keep this letter. It will save you a lot of time after our deaths.

If nothing else, remember this: Should you lose this letter, you will find an exact duplicate on my home computer. Turn the machine on, and it will automatically bring you to my computer desktop. On the desktop you'll find a file called "Estate Note." Open it, and there you'll find this letter.

Mom sends all her love, and so do I.

Daddy

THE BOTTOM LINE

You have an estate. When you die, it will either transfer to your survivors via your own plan or through a plan created for you by the courts. The consequences of not making a plan can prove catastrophic to your survivors.

A will is an essential part of any estate plan. It's a powerful instrument, but has some limitations. You will be able to make up for those limitations with trusts, life insurance, and gift giving. With an eye toward the goals of planning your estate, you must gather and review the documents that outline your current financial circumstances.

Charting the Course

Estate planning shouldn't be a ghoulish relay race during which you pass off your material possessions before your date with the grim reaper. Rather, planning your legacy often concerns what you can do today: giving gifts, buying insurance, and finding ways to make your assets grow. It's as much about maintaining your great-grandmother's memory by passing on her favorite pie plate to a beloved niece as it is determining who benefits from your life-insurance policy. You'll learn all about these issues later in the book. For now, though, you're probably most concerned about cash and cash equivalents. Fair enough.

How to Determine Your Worth . . . in Real Terms

Before you figure out what you want to give, and to whom you want to give it, you need to determine what you actually have.

Here's how to do it:

Sit down with a piece of paper and a pencil, and draw up a little chart. The headings should read:

• **What I Own:** Simple enough. List everything you own outright.

• **How I Own It:** Jot down how you hold title to certain property. (You'll learn more about this later in the chapter.)

• **Percentage Owned:** You may own all of your grandmother's diamond ring, half of your home, and one-third of your business.

• **Net Value:** The difference between the value of goods owned—most commonly, houses and cars—and the amount you still owe on them. If your home is worth $100,000, and you've got $30,000 left on the mortgage, the "net value" is $70,000.

Step 1:
What Do You Own?

You know you own "stuff." Stuff keeps cluttering up your attic and your garage. But the type of stuff you own—from life insurance and houses to automobiles and silverware—falls into one of the eight categories listed below. Examine these categories now. They will help jog your memory. You probably own more than you realize. Remember to write down the value of each item listed. This exercise may seem like a lot of work, but a few hours of planning now can save your loved ones trouble, financial hardship, and resentment later on.

Real Estate

Real estate is anything connected to land. Say you're the proprietor of a small business, one housed in an island cottage that you also own. The cottage is real estate. The business, its inventory, and other assets, are not.

Write down any real estate you own. Be spe-

F.Y.I.

Trusts & Estates magazine estimates that over the next few decades older Americans will pass on estates totaling, in aggregate, anywhere from $8 trillion to $10 trillion.

F.Y.I.

Should you hire an appraiser to find out how much your house is worth? If you bought it in the last few years, probably not. However, if you're not particularly familiar with local housing prices, call an area real estate agent. She may give you, as a courtesy, an idea of housing costs in your area. Pay for an appraiser only as a last resort.

cific. Don't just note "my house" or "the lot in New Hampshire." Instead, briefly describe each property: "Home on 1234 Maple Street, Anytown, Alabama" or "Vacant lot, RR 371, Lovely Place, Vermont." If there's any personal, not particularly valuable, property attached to the real estate—furniture, for example—expand your listing to read: "Home at 1234 Maple Drive, Anytown, Alabama, and all the furniture in it."

Underneath your description of the property, write its estimated net value; that is, its worth, minus what you owe on it.

Bank Accounts

Identify these clearly enough so that the probate judge, your lawyer, and your heirs will know exactly what you're talking about. Lots of people have multiple accounts in multiple banks. Therefore, make sure you identify yours properly. Note the amount of cash in each account—especially savings accounts. The list might read something like this:

• Checking, Bank of Greater New Hartfordville, Account No. 123-456-789.

• Savings, Keystone Bank, Philadelphia, Account No. 987-654-321.

• Savings, New York Greater Metropolitan Bank, Account No. 0123-04-0567

Personal Property

You probably don't really care about who gets your Beach Boys 8-tracks, your 12-year-old lawnmower, or the bike you picked up cheap at a garage sale. But you should list any personal property with financial or sentimental value. This list can include *everything*, from the your great-grandmother's personal diaries to the same lady's two-carat heirloom diamond.

Consider hiring an appraiser to determine the financial worth of any personal property that may have monetary value. If your great-grandfather collected Hummel figurines, you don't want an uninformed grandchild selling that collection at a garage sale for a buck a statuette after you're gone.

Stocks, Bonds, Money Market Accounts, Mutual Funds

If you keep your stocks at home, list exactly where your heirs can find them; for example, "Top drawer, gray filing cabinet, stored in my home office on 123 Main Street."

If you employ an outside manager to handle your assets, note the name of the firm and your account number: "All stocks and any other assets are held in Account Number 1234-5678, at John Doe & Co., Cleveland, Ohio."

If you don't know the current value or exact number of an account, call your broker, banker, or money manager and ask him to send you a copy of your records.

SMART DEFINITION

Real property
Real estate

Anything connected to land.

Personal property

Anything else you own, from the cash in your bank account to your family photo albums.

An Example:

If you own a mobile home, do you consider it real estate or personal property? That depends. If it's attached to a particular lot, it's real estate. If it's either parked in your garage or toting the family and grandparents to Yellowstone, it's personal property.

SMART SOURCES

You can find appraisers listed in the Yellow Pages of any city. But if you want an accredited professional, consider checking out the American Society of Appraisers. Members of this organization can determine the value of your business, jewelry, heavy machinery, personal property, and real estate. You can search for an appraiser in your area by logging on to the organization's web site at www.appraisers.org, or by phone at (800) ASA-VALU.

Insurance Policies and Pension Funds

For insurance, list the policy number and the name of your insurance company. For pensions, list the kind of pension, its number, and company name.

Vehicles

List all vehicles by name and title/registration and license numbers. Jot down their approximate value.

Business Interests

Note here the value of any business you own or have proprietary interest in—not including the building in which it sits; if you own the building, list it under real estate—and any partnerships you have joined.

You can list any businesses you own by name only. If you own a part of an operation, you should note, "My 30 percent interest in Harry's Recycling" or "My 15 percent share of Joe's Butcher Shop." Include an address and telephone number for each corporation.

Determining Worth

It's easy to determine the worth of your car—any bookstore stocks the *Blue Book,* the bible of automobile valuation. You know how much cash you've stashed in your savings account—the bank sends you a statement each month.

But what about your other possessions? You bought your house for $150,000 ten years ago. What's a fair market price now? Has it risen or fallen?

And those antique plates that your great-grandmother left you? Are they worth anything beyond their sentimental value? Or your original Beatles records? Or a first edition of John Steinbeck's *The Grapes of Wrath?*

You just don't know what these goods are worth. You need to hire an appraiser—a professional who will put a price on the property you own.

First, let's took a look at what you might need appraised.

This determination is largely a matter of common sense. The lamps you bought at Wal-Mart five years ago have not gone up in value. Nor has your new IKEA furniture. The fake pearls you received for Christmas are still fake pearls. They're worth no more now than at the time of purchase.

What do you need to hire an appraiser for, then? Anything expensive, or anything old. These items include:

- **Your house.** Real estate appraisers will determine its current value.

- **Your jewelry.** You should appraise any expensive jewelry you own (gold, diamonds, emeralds, and others). The sheer craftsmanship of your grandmother's gold-and-garnet ring may make it valuable, regardless of the worth of its metal and gem.

- **Your art and collectibles.** Hire an appraiser to examine any original pieces you own, and any significant lithographs. Your collection of Steuben glass could also use a look, along with your Lennox gee-gaws and Hummel figurines. And those first editions cramming your library may be worth a bundle.

- **Your antiques.** Ask a professional to examine any antiques in your home, from your rolltop desk to your grandmother's china.

- **Your artifacts from pop culture.** If you're a pack rat, and have actually kept, in good condition, your vintage baseball-card collection, your original Spiderman comics, and toys left in their original wrapping, call in a pro to determine their worth.

Patents, Copyrights, and Royalties

Identify patents by the patent number and title. Identify copyright and royalties by the title of the relevant material.

Step 2: What Do You Owe?

In determining the net worth of your home and cars, you've already taken into consideration amounts still owing to the bank for your mortgage and loans. Now it's time to list other debts as well. On a separate sheet of paper, write down all those credit card debts, the loan you incurred from your Uncle Seymour, and anything else you owe to anyone else.

Step 3: How Do I Own It? How Much of It Do I Own?

If you're single and you own all your property on your own, you don't have to worry about how you hold title to your property.

But, by the time you actually worry about planning your estate, you've probably reached a point in your life when you're "partnered" with someone else. You and your best buddy may have started a successful law firm. You may have taken a spouse or a life partner.

These people own a percentage of at least some of your stuff. And the person who probably has the surest claim to your estate is your spouse.

You Said, "I Do": Marriage and Property

In the United States, getting married means that you've agreed to share a portion of your worldly goods with someone. Divorce lawyers can haggle over distribution of property if you and your once-beloved call off your relationship while you're still both living. But if while married one partner dies, the survivor will inherit something. In every state, he or she *will inherit something*.

Why It Matters Where You Live: Community Property and Common Law States

If you live in the United States, the ownership of your property can be determined by whether you live in a community property state or a common law state, and each of the fifty states is one or the other.

Community Property States

Arizona, California, Idaho, Louisiana, Nevada, New Mexico, Texas, Washington, and Wisconsin

F.Y.I.

You can save time if you and your spouse sit down together to plan your estate. The process will run much more smoothly if you both agree on whom should get what.

Also, know this: You and your spouse may have mutually agreed that all your assets pass to the other upon one partner's death. But that's not enough. Any highway patrolman can tell you that married couples die simultaneously all the time. It's not enough for you and your husband to leave each other all your goods. You need to have a backup plan.

Do You Live in a Community Property State or a Common Law State?

State	Community Property	Common Law	State	Community Property	Common Law
Alabama		*	Missouri		*
Alaska		*	Montana		*
Arizona	*		Nebraska		*
Arkansas		*	Nevada	*	
California	*		New Hampshire		*
Colorado		*	New Jersey		*
Connecticut		*	New Mexico	*	
Delaware		*	New York		*
District of Columbia		*	North Carolina		*
Florida		*	North Dakota		*
Georgia		*	Ohio		*
Hawaii		*	Oklahoma		*
Idaho	*		Oregon		*
Illinois		*	Pennsylvania		*
Indiana		*	Rhode Island		*
Iowa		*	South Carolina		*
Kansas		*	South Dakota		*
Kentucky		*	Tennessee		*
Louisiana	*		Texas	*	
Maine		*	Utah		*
Maryland		*	Vermont		*
Massachusetts		*	Virginia		*
Michigan		*	Washington	*	
Minnesota		*	West Virginia		*
Mississippi		*	Wisconsin	*	
			Wyoming		*

have mandated that everything two people earn or buy after saying "I do" belongs equally to both spouses. Anything you owned before marriage—including real estate or cash deposited in bank accounts—can be kept out of the family pot.

Common Law States

All the remaining states have mandated that for the course of a married couple's lives, "What's mine stays mine and what's yours stays yours. But if the marriage ends in death, I have to leave you one-third to one-half my stuff, depending on the state in which we live."

Below you'll learn about all the different ways you can hold title to property. All this information must be viewed in the context of your marriage and the state in which you live.

Think of it this way: You and a buddy went out, a few years back, and bought a $50,000 sailboat. You each own half of it, so your share of the sailboat is worth $25,000. You want to leave that share to your mistress. But, if you live in a community property state, you can't will her $25,000 worth of sailboat. Your wife legally owns half of your share. Therefore, the best you can do for your lady friend is a one-quarter ownership of the whole boat, or $12,500 worth.

Taking Possession: Holding Title to Property

There are four basic ways to hold title to property. The property can be your marital home, your business, your hunting cottage, or anything else of

F.Y.I.

There are certain exceptions to community property laws. Some goods received over the course of a marriage can be held by only one partner if:

• The property is a bequest willed solely to one partner.

• Both partners say—legally and in writing—that they want a given asset to be held by one spouse only.

States Allowing Tenancy by the Entirety

Arkansas

District of Columbia

Florida

Hawaii

Maryland

Massachusetts

Michigan

Mississippi

Missouri

New York

North Carolina

Ohio

Oregon

Pennsylvania

Rhode Island

Tennessee

Vermont

Virginia

Wyoming

value that you have purchased with another human being—not just your spouse. The four title types include:

1. Joint Tenancy with the Right of Survivorship

Two or more people holding title as joint tenants with the right of survivorship agree that, if one tenant dies, his share automatically passes to the remaining partner or partners.

This is a popular type of ownership because it bypasses probate. Say you own a home with your spouse as joint tenants with the right of survivorship. Once he dies, the entire house automatically passes into your hands. Your right to your spouse's share of this domicile does not need to be okayed by a probate judge.

Joint tenancy can be used by any group.

2. Tenancy by the Entirety

Tenancy by the entirety is a form of ownership similar to joint tenancy. However, it is only available to married couples and only in 19 states. Like joint tenancy, property owned by tenants in entirety does not go to probate court after the death of one tenant—it simply passes into the hands of the other.

This form of ownership also provides protection against creditors. Creditors can not attach a property owned by tenants in the entirety unless both partners have incurred the debt. Consider this scenario: Your husband is sued by his ex-wife for $25,000 in back child support. She wins. But your husband doesn't have $25,000. If you and your spouse own your home under tenancy by the entirety, his ex cannot attach it for payment of that judgment—because the judgment was levied against him only, not both marital partners.

Creditors can attach your property only if you divorce, or if the property is sold.

3. Tenancy In Common

Two or more persons own shares of a property. The shares need not be equal and each tenant can will his shares to whomever he likes. Let's say you and your brother inherited from your dad a family vacation cottage in Maine. You own it as tenants-in-common. You can will your half of the cottage to your descendants. Your brother can do what he likes with his half.

4. Sole Ownership

You own it on your own. Can apply even to married people in community property states. Say your great-grandfather didn't much like your husband, Sam. He may have decided to leave you the ancestral estate up in San Francisco, pointedly leaving Sam out of his bequest. That house belongs to you, and you alone.

SMART SOURCES

If you don't remember offhand how you and your husband decided to take title to your home when you bought it back in 1973, that's okay. To determine how you own property, check the following records:

Real estate: Deed

Car and other vehicles: Certificate of title or registration

Bank accounts: Passbook or registration card held at the bank

Stocks and bonds: Stock certificates

Insurance policy: Policy records

Step 4: Doing the Math: Figuring Net Value and Net Worth

So far, you've listed your real estate and its value, your personal property and its value, and what percentage of which asset is actually yours to bequeath.

Now it's just time to plug the numbers into the chart.

Jan J., 56, married, and a resident of California (everyone's favorite community property state), is compiling her own chart. Even though she lives in a community property state, she knows that she has goods that she has accrued on her own—goods that her partner has no right to touch. And, of course, she has assets that she owns together with her husband.

When Jan adds starts adding up the "net value" column, she learns that her estate is worth $609,000. She then writes down any outstanding debts she has—the amount still owing on the house and cars covered above, but not her credit card debts. The total is $6,000. She subtracts that total from the $609,000 and comes up with her net worth, $603,000.

But remember, Jan is married, and some of her property—including half the cash in her bank accounts and half the value of their cars—must pass, by law, to Bill. In addition, by holding their marital home as joint tenant, the couple has decided that the entire house will pass to the remaining spouse. Finally, Bill is responsible for half of the marital credit card debts.

Sample Assets/Net Worth Chart

What I Own	How I Own It	Percentage Owned	Net Value
Home 1234 Maple Ave. Los Angeles	Joint tenancy, with Bill	50%	Property value: $175,000 Mortgage owing: 25,000 Net value: $150,000
Grandfather's house 3333 E. Lake Road Shoretown, CA	Sole owner	100%	Property value: $225,000 Mortgage owing: 0 Net value: $225,000
1996 Volvo, Tag No.: CA. 3672	In common, with Bill	50%	Value: $18,000 Loan still owed: $6,000 Net value: $12,000
1998 Honda Accord Tag No.: CA. 8722	In common, with Bill	50%	Valued at: $19,000 Loan still owed: $3,000 Net value: $16,000
Greater L.A. Savings Bank Savings Acct., No. 6538	In common, with Bill	50%	Net value: $73,000
Bank of San Diego, Checking Acct., No. 778654	In common, with Bill	50%	Net value: $19,000
Grandmother's Waterford crystal collection	Sole owner	100%	Net value: $7,000
Pierce-Lehman Brokerage San Fran., Acct. No. 887293	In common, with Bill	50%	Net value: $100,000
Grandmother's diamond ring, in safe-deposit box at Greater L.A. Savings Bank	Sole owner	100%	Net value: $7,000

The assets that Jan can distribute on her own—including bequests from her grandparents, left to her solely—have a net value of $349,000. Subtract from that half the marital credit card debts and voilà! Her personal, "distribute-able" net worth is $346,000.

The Worst Case: An Estate in the Red

Some readers will add up their assets and their debts and see that the latter outweighs the former.

What to do?

First, don't panic. The afterlife has no telephone lines or roadways accessible by earthlings. Your creditors truly can't touch you.

And you know that. You may, however, worry about how the bills that trickle in, and sometimes flood in, after your death will affect your loved ones.

Your spouse will continue to be responsible for debts you incurred jointly—the house, the car, and all others.

But if you are the second spouse to die, what will your children and other loved ones owe your creditors?

Nothing at all.

After your death, banks will want the money you still owe on your house and your car. Your credit card companies will wonder where your monthly payment has gone to. Hospitals will want their balances paid. The electric company and phone company will send out their monthly bills as usual.

"What I Own" Worksheet

Use this worksheet to determine your assets and the "total net value" of what you own. The total net value of your goods is your "estate." Make photocopies if additional space is needed.

What I Own	How I Own It	Percentage Owned	Net Value

Total Net Value: _____

You owed this money. After your death, those debts will be passed on to your estate. Banks might repossess, if no one is paying what you owed on the car and the house. Credit card companies and other creditors may place liens against your estate. But you had nothing to leave in the first place. These organizations are pretty much out of luck.

Your good-hearted and responsible children may feel compelled, when faced with mounting debts, to start paying them off themselves. This is absolutely unnecessary—and unfair. They didn't incur these debts. You did. Their failure to make good on what you owe will in no way (despite what some overzealous collection agencies may say) affect their own credit histories. Every large lending corporation includes a substantial line item in the "expenditures" section of its annual budget for write-offs, or uncollectible debts. Yours will be one of these.

What about your funeral? In a worst-case scenario, local governments take charge of interring the bodies of the indigent. But you probably don't want that. Inexpensive funeral arrangements are discussed in chapter 8.

Help Wanted: Hiring Estate Professionals

You've determined what you have to leave. Now you have to spend some time figuring out who gets what, and through which estate vehicles your assets will be doled out. Depending on the size of your estate, the process can be a bit complicated. You may need a professional hand.

As you plan your estate, you may find that your legacy is larger, and perhaps more complicated, than you originally thought. The size of your estate may mean that your loved ones will be hit by a hefty estate-tax levy, unless you take advantage of certain trusts and other tax-avoidance techniques. But you have no idea how to go about implementing these plans.

Take heart. Everyone needs help sometimes. You may want to assemble an estate-planning team. Its members are listed below. You probably won't need all these pros on your side. You can just hire those who specialize in your specific estate needs.

Estate Planners

These are financial planners with special training in estates. They can help you determine how you can best organize your legacy. They will give you valuable information on which trusts and other estate-planning tools will best provide for the financial support of your heirs.

Estate Lawyers

These legal professionals plan estates and can also draft the accompanying necessary legal documents. In contrast with an estate planner, who may know just the trust that is suited to your needs, the estate lawyer knows how to draft the documents that create the trust to ensure that all your issues and contingencies are covered.

SMART SOURCES

Looking for a qualified estate planner? The National Association of Estate Planners and Councils runs a strict accrediting program for its members. You can search for accredited planners by state on the organization's web site:

http://naepc.org/

You can also telephone the Bryn Mawr, Pennsylvania, association at:

(610) 526-1389

Insurance Agents

Not just someone you'd search out for car insurance, these agents will sell you policies that can help ensure the continued support of your family—including getting them the cash they will likely need immediately following your death. To learn about the different types of policies that may be useful in estate planning, see chapter 6.

Appraisers

As noted above, these specialists will give you a handle on property whose worth you question—everything from your home and property to your classic Thunderbird to your grandmother's string of black pearls.

Charitable Trust Executives

Sound advice can be had from these executives if you need help in determining how donations to a good cause can help minimize your tax levy, assuming your planned bequest is large enough. In general, the greater the assets you're considering donating to a charitable trust, the more helpful you'll find these executives to be.

Bank Trust Officers

These banking professionals will help you set up the trusts discussed in chapter 4. These folks can also serve as your trustees; that is, the people in charge of managing trust assets. For more information on trusts and trustees, see chapter 5.

How to Choose a Financial Planner

You can use the same basic routine to choose a financial planner as you would to find a doctor or a lawyer. First, compile a list of planners by asking for recommendations from friends, relatives, colleagues, your accountant or lawyer, or through advertisements, newspapers, or magazine articles. Call several names from this list to find about more about his or her professional background.

Good financial planners usually have a fiscal or legal background, with professional training and experience in accounting, banking or finance, insurance, stocks and securities, or tax law. Their titles often are a clue to their specialties. There are certified financial planners, certified public accountants, and chartered life underwriters (insurance specialists). A chartered financial consultant typically comes from an insurance background. Most planners are accredited, but no matter what their title, remember that competence and quality varies from individual to individual. That's why it's important to set up a face-to-face interview and get more specific information about any planner you're considering.

What's in a Name: The ABCs of Financial Certification

The following are some handy definitions to help you make sense of the alphabet soup of financial professionals.

Accredited Estate Planner (AEP). The National Association of Estate Planners and Counselors in Bryn Mawr, Pennsylvania, administers an exam for prospective financial planners, who then receive this name.

Chartered Financial Analyst (CFA). The Association for Investment Management and Research (AIMR) in Charlottesville, Virginia, certifies that a chartered financial analyst has three years experience in stock analysis and money management, has passed three AIMR exams, and abides by the AIMR professional and ethical code.

Certified Financial Planner (CFP). A Certified Financial Planner has a bachelor's degree and three years of financial planning experience. Candidates must also pass an exam given by the Certified Financial Planner Board of Standards in Denver, Colorado, in addition to taking financial planning courses at a college or university. To maintain the CFP, planners must continue to take 30 hours of coursework every two years and sign an annual disclosure statement regarding ethical conduct.

Chartered Life Underwriter (CLU). This professional designation is given to those who have three years of business experience and agree to comply with the Code of Ethics and procedures of The American College in Bryn Mawr, Pennsylvania. Candidates must also take 10 courses in estate planning, financial planning, group benefits, income taxes, investments, life insurance, and retirement planning.

Chartered Financial Consultant (ChFC). Also awarded by the American College to those who have already earned the Chartered Life Underwriter certification and who take three additional courses: financial decision making at retirement, financial planning applications, and wealth accumulation planning.

Chartered Mutual Fund ConsultantSM (CMFC). The National Endowment for Financial Education in Denver, Colorado, and the Investment Company Institute in Washington, D.C., administer a nine-section home-study course, a proctored final exam, and a code of ethics to planners who want this designation.

Certified Public Accountant (CPA). A CPA has to pass a national examination and also be certified in the state in which he or she practices. CPAs specialize in accounting and state and federal tax laws.

Enrolled Agent (EA). A tax preparer who has passed an exam given by the Internal Revenue Service and who continue to take tax classes throughout their careers.

National Association of Financial and Estate Planning Certified Estate Advisor (NCEA). For people who are trained and who pass a test administered by NAFEP, based in Salt Lake City, Utah. An NCEA can help set up trusts and other more complicated estate matters.

Personal Financial Specialist (PFS). American Institute of Certified Public Accountants (AICPA) members who have a college education in accounting and finance, on-the-job training under a CPA's supervision, and who have passed an exam administered by the AICPA can become a Personal Financial Specialist.

Registered Financial Consultant (RFC). The International Association of Registered Financial Consultants in St. Louis, Missouri, offers a training program and gives this certification to those who pass its exam.

Fees for Financial Planning

Financial planners may bill you using one of three different fee structures: commission-based, hourly fee–based, and per project. In addition to general planning, a commission-based planner is in the business of selling investments such as stocks. He or she then earns a commission on whatever sales are made. Fee-based planners don't sell anything but their service. They submit a flat-fee bill based either on the number of hours they worked with or for you, or on a specific project. According to the American Institute of Certified Financial Planners Board of Standards, fees range from $500 to $10,000, depending on the project.

Questions to Ask a Financial Planner

When you're interviewing a potential financial planner, the following questions can be useful:

• What are your credential and degrees?

• How do you bill? Is it a fee or commission? A combination?

• May I get a printed schedule of costs from you before I hire you?

• Is there any way you can help me reduce my financial planning costs?

• Can you describe your background in financial planning? How did you get involved in it? Did you do something else before?

- Do you work primarily with businesses or large companies or with individuals?

- Would you work with my attorney and accountant so that my financial plan is most efficient?

- May I have a list of references?

Budget Legal Help

A good estate plan definitely requires a sound legal architect. You want your plan to have a solid foundation—and to stand up in court. But if you're working within a limited income, you don't necessarily have to pay top dollar for a competent lawyer. There are several low-cost alternatives:

Pro Bono Programs

Many private law firms have informal sliding scales for lower-income clients. They are willing to offer their services for reduced fees according to the ability of the individual to pay. Known as pro bono work—meaning for the good of the community— these programs are sometimes publicly listed with bar associations. Others are available only unofficially, and you simply have to ask. Call first the largest firms you can find. Then describe very specifically the type of legal help you need and ask whether the firm offers any kind of pro bono financial arrangement. For example: "My wife and I need to draw up a will to provide guardians for our children. We're living on a limited income. Could your firm help us through any sort of pro bono program?"

State and Local Bar Associations

Bar associations often sponsor legal programs, such as Neighborhood Legal Services Clinics, which provide advice for nominal fees or even gratis. Check in your local telephone directory under "Lawyer Referral Service."

Nonprofit Legal Services

Your community may have a legal office, funded either with government money or privately. Before you can use these nonprofit offices, you usually have to pass specific tests for financial eligibility.

All in the Family: Bequething Your Legacy

Before you start making specific bequests to specific loved ones, take a few quiet minutes for yourself. Curl up by the fire or linger over your morning coffee, and think about what you want to achieve with what you've accumulated. What do you want to do for the people you love? What type of bequest would most help them fulfill their goals?

When you write a will and plan your estate, you're putting your money where your heart is. So it's important to listen to what your heart has to

F.Y.I.

Get out a pen and sheet of paper and write down the names of your 20 favorite people or 20 favorite people and charitable organizations. Think of what you want to do for each and jot down your dream bequests. This process gets the estate-planning ball rolling.

say. If you want to give your seven-year-old nephew a sound start in life, you may think of putting money in trust for his college education. If you worry that your hard-working but money-strapped daughter and son-in-law face an uncomfortable old age, you might want to set up a trust fund for their retirement. And, of course, you still have to figure out to whom you want to give your most treasured knick-knacks and gee-gaws.

Map out your dream bequests now on a worksheet based on the following model. (You can always worry about the dollars and cents later.)

I Want to Bequeath a Legacy To . . .	His/Her Dream Is . . .	I Can Help Fulfill It By . . .
My nephew, Benny	To become a lawyer	Tax-free gifts made in direct payment of his tuition
My sister, Emily	To open an antiques shop	Giving her Grandma's antique china and cutlery for display
The City Humane Society	To stop euthanizing healthy animals	Leave a trust for a free spay/neuter program

Before deciding what you want to give to whom, remember this: Unless your family and friends know about your estate plans, they will naturally see your gift as a measure of your love. Let's say you have a $125,000 estate. In your will, you leave your daughter $50,000 and your son $75,000.

Don't be penny wise and pound foolish. Don't get so wrapped up in listing family gee-gaws that you forget to tell your heirs about your stocks.

A contrary millionaire named Harry J. left a will carefully spelling out which loved one should get each one of his Montovani records and cowboy bolo ties. He failed, however, to list his out-of-state bank accounts—accounts in which he'd stashed the bulk of his fortune. His wife knew he had them. She just didn't know where. As a result, some banks—his wife thinks Texas banks—made out very well after Harry J. died. His family and friends . . . they're still listening to Montovani and wearing the ties.

You chose unequal bequests because ten years ago you gave your daughter $25,000 as a down payment on a new home. Your son never needed that type of help during your lifetime.

You think you're treating two equally loved children absolutely equally. But, if you fail to discuss your plans and rationale with them, sometime, during the course of probate, your daughter will lean over to your son and say, "I always knew Mom loved you best." Count on it.

How to Ensure That Your Legacy Won't Cause Resentment

More than one family has argued bitterly over the estate of a parent or another loved one. Often family members don't feel the legacy they received was fair. Cousin Martha feels that she should have gotten at least as much from your estate as Cousin Roger. Your daughter may have "forgotten" the $15,000 car you bought her in 1997 and wonder why her brother's final bequest ran $15,000 more than hers. To avoid fallout over your estate, you should:

Talk It Out

Discuss your plans with your heirs. You'll uncover small problems that will fester if left unaddressed. Families have fallen apart over Great-grandma's crystal or Dad's baseball cards. You can prevent family rancor by discussing your plans with your heirs now.

Listen, Too

Tell your heirs about your plans, then listen to their reactions. Don't interrupt, even if your niece Cindy starts to question your well-laid plans. You may expect her to jump for joy after you tell her of your decision to leave her $5,000. She may tell you that she'd much prefer her grandmother's Victorian sofa. It's a piece of furniture valued at about five grand. No one else in your family has much use for it. You may well want to give Cindy the sofa and bequeath $5,000 in cash to someone else.

When Necessary, Hold Your Peace

For all today's talk of openness and communication, sometimes silence is perfectly adequate. Do you really have to tell your brother and only sibling that in the event of your death your two minor children are going directly to your best fried? It depends. If you have a close relationship and can discuss your rationale openly, terrific. You may want to say, "Tommy, my estate isn't worth too much, and I know that you and Susie are just making ends meet right now. I always want you to know and love and spend time with my kids, but I don't want them to be a financial burden."

If, however, you've decided to pack the kids off to your best friend's home because your big brother has a nasty habit of beating his wife—silence does just fine.

If Possible, Give Equally

Lots of families do this, and it works out just fine. A widowed mom has $200,000 to leave. She bequests half to her son, half to her daughter—all clean, easy, legal, and neat.

WHAT MATTERS, WHAT DOESN'T

What Matters

• Realizing it's *your* plan, and you have every right to give whatever you want to whomever you want.

• Devising and implementing an overall estate plan.

• Frank communication with your heirs.

• Knowing that your decisions were made out of a sense of love and fairness.

What Doesn't

• Trying to shape your estate plan to accommodate your loved ones' wishes.

• That people may or may not understand your rationale in your decisions.

But suppose the daughter and her husband are struggling to raise three children on a teacher's salary, and the son is a single executive at a Very Large Company, pulling down a quarter million a year, to say nothing of stock options?

If the mother has a good relationship with her son, she may want to have a private chat with him. She can explain that she loves him beyond measure but that his sister just seems to need the money more than he does. With any luck, he'll say, "Mom, I understand."

Tag It!

While you're still hale and hearty, host a "tag" party for your heirs. Have everyone over, go through your home, determine who gets what of sentimental value, and tag each item with your loved one's name. That way, when your survivors take possession of your old digs, they'll know immediately which treasured possession goes to whom.

You'll learn more about passing on your two most important assets—your family business and your home—in chapter 7.

Deciding Whether to Disinherit Someone

You have an adult child who's lifestyle or moral code you do not approve of. In fact, you are quite angry with this child because of the way he's chosen to manage his life. Maybe he's living with his lover, rather than marrying her, as your religion mandates. Maybe he's a drug abuser. Maybe he beats his wife. Maybe he just doesn't call on Mother's Day.

Should you disinherit this child? You can, if you want. No law mandates that you must leave part of your estate to an adult child. The decision is yours.

But, generally, disinheriting a child is a bad idea. Look at the following scenario:

Say you're a widower with a $300,000 estate and three adult children. Both your daughters work hard, lead responsible lives, and do the best they can, all around. Your only son, Bobby, is a cocaine addict.

Disinheriting Bobby virtually ensures a court battle over your legacy. Bobby may or may not win, but he will surely keep your estate in the hands of the courts—and out of the hands of your daughters—while the case drags on.

Second, the disinheritance will likely destroy any relationship between Bobby and his sisters. It will cause bitter rows among family members after your death. That is one legacy you surely don't want to leave.

Leaving Bobby some type of reasonable inheritance will likely forestall such court battles and help keep the family peace after your death. You can leave him considerably less than you leave your daughters, but enough so he'll think twice about squandering the amount he's been given on lawyers' fees.

Or, you may decide to leave your daughters $100,000 each, free and clear, and put Bobby's share in a trust to be doled out piecemeal—say, $1,000 a month. You've made this decision because you don't want your death to finance your son's overdose. Or you may take an even stronger stance—leaving Bobby $100,000 with the stipula-

STREET SMARTS

Roberta Q. loves animals. She spends most Sundays bathing oil-soaked birds and walking stray dogs. She has come up with a plan that will pay her a dividend for the rest of her life, save her money on taxes, and take care of her beloved wildlife and strays when she dies.

She has set up a "charitable trust" with her local Humane Society.

Roberta remains the beneficiary of the trust during her lifetime. But when she dies, the principal passes, tax-and-probate-free, to the cause dearest to her heart. See the next chapter for more information on trusts.

tion that a percentage of it be used to pay for his stay in a drug-treatment center, the rest becoming his after he has been clean for a year.

For information on various trusts, see the following chapter and chapter 7.

Providing for Your Best (Four-Legged) Friend

While the idea may seem unimportant to some, many older people worry about who will take care their beloved household pets after they, the owners, die.

There are two simple solutions. You can bequeath the animal to a trusted relative or friend. And, since you don't want your dog or cat to become a financial burden to another loved one, you should leave you animal's guardian, outright, an amount sufficient to care for the animal's food, routine veterinary care, kennel board for when the new owners go on vacation, and extraordinary veterinary care should Fido ever need surgery—for the rest of his life.

This is how you do it. You have a five-year-old golden retriever named Sandy. You wish her a good, long life, so we'll say she'll live to be about 15. You have determined that the cost of her regular yearly expenses—food, routine health care, and board (you go on vacation for two weeks a year, her new owners probably will, as well)—run about $1,100 annually. Multiply 1,100 by 10 years (the dog's projected remaining life span) and you come up with $11,000. As Sandy ages, she may also need some extraordinary veterinary care, so you take on another few thousand to cover that contingency. You leave, in your will, $15,000 outright to Sandy's new guardian.

Of course, no matter how much you love and trust Sandy's new owner, in this scenario you have no guarantee that he will actually use the cash you've willed for Sandy's care. What to do?

Believe it or not, you can set up a trust for an animal. Sandy would be your beneficiary, and you would name a party other than Sandy's guardian as trustee. The trustee would dole out money at regular intervals for Sandy's continuing care and check up on the dog occasionally to make sure that the money is being used for that purpose. (For explanation of trusts, see chapter 5.)

Of course, you want to take great care in naming a new guardian for your beloved pet. A pet should never be a "surprise" legacy. You should talk to potential guardians at length about their willingness and ability to care for your animal. In general, you want someone you trust, someone who wants to care for your pet, and someone who is able to care for your pet. If your dog just loves his daily two-mile jog, you probably don't want to leave him to a housebound best friend.

Storing Your Documents

Now you should have a handle on what you own, how you own it, and what you plan to give to whom. You've written down all this information.

THE BOTTOM LINE

Take some time now to calculate your net worth, taking into account whether you own a given asset as a joint tenant, tenant-in-common, or sole owner. If you live in a community property state, your spouse, by law, controls half the marital assets. Hire any professionals that you need for help. Frank discussions with your heirs will help avoid interfamilial squabbles over your legacy. Disinherit a child only if absolutely necessary.

And remember: This is your life. These are your goods. This is your legacy. Trust yourself.

Keep your notes in a safe place. You'll need them as you decide which vehicles—wills, trusts, or others—you want to use to pass on your assets.

This is the perfect time, in fact, to decide on a safe place to store all your estate-planning documents. Gathering necessary paperwork in one locale will save your loved ones an irritating game of "find the forms" after your death. You may choose a bank safe-deposit box, an office filing cabinet, or a fireproof lock box you keep in your bedroom closet. It doesn't really matter. What does matter is that your heirs know where they can find the appropriate estate information.

It's Your Deal

In the end, it's your plan. In the end, you have every right to give whatever you want to whomever you want. People may or may not understand your rationale, but you know that your decisions are made out of a sense of love and fairness. Be frank in communicating with your heirs, but don't feel you must shape your estate plan to accommodate your every loved one's every wish.

Devising and implementing an overall estate plan is what matters—and the building blocks of this plan exist in the following chapters.

....

Death and . . . You Know

By the year 2006, you can leave an estate valued at $1 million, and the federal government won't tax it a dime.

The bad news is, $1 million isn't worth as much as it used to be.

And the real news is that the value of the average American's estate is worth not much more than the value of a small house, a couple of used cars, and a few thousand in savings. All the more reason to plan carefully for yourself and your heirs, no matter what the value of your estate.

Are You Likely to Be a Millionaire?

You may be a 37-year-old executive making $65,000 per year. You think that the chances of your ever having to worry about estate taxes are nil. There's simply no way you'll have more than $1 million to leave.

Think again.

Let's assume your parents die within the next few years, leaving you $350,000. Your personal estate then consists of your parents' $350,000 legacy; $67,000 in cash assets that you've saved over the years; a home with a net value of $125,000; and—this is the kicker—a $750,000 life insurance policy. Your estate now totals $1.29 million. If you die suddenly, say, in 2009, the government will tax $290,000 of your estate. Why? You've gone over the million-dollar estate credit allowed by Uncle Sam. The tax rate on $290,000 is 34 percent. Your estate will end up paying a total of $98,600 to the federal government.

Trevor is a case in point. He is a young lawyer. His mom died some time ago, and his father passed away in 1997, leaving him $500,000 in cash as well as a house. Because the estate exceeded the $600,000 tax-credit cap for that year, Trevor ended up paying $350,000 in taxes and selling the house at a loss.

Trevor's father was a good man, but his poor estate-planning techniques resulted in a heavy tax burden for his son.

Federal Taxes

In 1997, the U.S. government passed a law increasing the amount individuals can leave in their estates before those estates become subject to federal taxation.

The increase takes effect gradually. Here's a schedule:

If You Die In	Your Estate Won't Be Subject to Federal Taxation If It Totals No More Than
1999	$650,000
2000–2001	$675,000
2002–2003	$700,000
2004	$850,000
2005	$950,000
2006 or later	$1 million

Estates totaling more than the amounts listed above are subject to both federal and state taxation. Don't fret, though. Here, and in the following chapters, you'll find legitimate ways to minimize your tax liability.

As noted in chapter 2, when considering the size of your estate, don't think in terms of just cash assets and real estate. Your total estate consists of cash and cash equivalents, real estate, pensions, life insurance policies, personal property, and anything else you can think of.

For Those of Modest Means

Many readers, using chapter 2 as a guide, have tallied up their assets and outstanding debts and determined that their total estate now falls below the estate-tax credit set by the federal government. If you are in this position—well, it's terrific, in a way. You don't have to worry about planning your estate to avoid federal taxation. (Of course, you'll still want to read all about trusts and other vehicles that avoid probate to give your heirs immediate access to your assets.) If, however, you're a little disappointed with the size of your estate and would like to have to worry about avoiding taxes, take heart. It's never too late to start saving. Check out books such as the *Smart Guide to Personal Finance* to learn how to grow your legacy.

Tax Types

Depending on where you live and how much your estate totals, the wealth you leave behind may be subject to three different types of taxes. Here's a list.

Unified Gift and Estate Tax

In 1997, Congress passed the Unified Gift and Estate Tax law. The law is an attempt to equally tax the transfer of wealth, whether the transfer occurs during the giver's lifetime or after his death.

The law calls for federal-tax exclusions in the amounts listed above. It also allows single persons to give annual tax-free gifts of up to $10,000 per year to anyone they choose. Married couples may give up to $20,000 per year, tax free, to anyone they like.

If, however, a single person gives more than $10,000 to any one person during the course of a calendar year, the excess will be deducted from the amount he may leave, tax free, in his estate. The same holds true for a married couple giving more than $20,000.

This is how it works. You are a single man. In 2001, you give your favorite nephew $2,000 to purchase a used car. You die in 2003—when the estate-credit cap is $700,000. Since you gave a single $2,000 gift during one calendar year, only the first $698,000 of your estate will be exempt from federal taxation—that is, $700,000 thousand dollars minus the "extra" $2,000 you gave to your nephew in 2001.

Smart Moves to Avoid the Tax

You'll find some exceptions to this rule. You can make unlimited gifts to an individual in a single calendar year without affecting your estate credit if you:

• Make the gift in direct payment of a medical bill.

SMART MONEY

In February 1999, *USA Today* reported that President Clinton's budget proposal for fiscal 2000 could heavily tax estates worth more than $17 million, by disallowing the estate-tax credits offered to smaller legacies. This means that if you die in 2007, leaving $17 million, the federal government would levy taxes against your entire estate, without the $1 million credit available to everyone else. Therefore, if you are leaving a particularly large legacy, you need to make doubly certain that you employ legal means to avoid federal tax levies. Talk with a qualified lawyer.

SMART SOURCES

The renowned accounting firm of Deloitte & Touche offers a web site listing the firm's take on estate taxes and how to avoid them.

http://www.dtonline.com/taxguide98/changes1.htm

SMART SOURCES

Anytime you give anyone, in a single calendar year, a gift worth more than $10,000, you must report the transfer to the IRS. You can download IRS. Form 706 from the service's web site.

http://www.irs.gov./

• Make the gift in direct payment of a tuition bill. This exception applies to tuition bills only, not all the amenities of going to college. For example, it does not apply to dorm rental fees, college meal plans, or the purchase of textbooks. Still, this deduction can be a terrific estate-planning tool. If your estate sits somewhere on the border of being taxed, draw it down now by paying, say, your granddaughter's tuition bills.

"I've given my children and grandchildren the thing I cared about most," says Sandra, a retired bank employee. "I gave them an education. I went to college during the Depression, and I had to drop out in the middle and earn my way back. I decided the nicest thing I could give them was an education, debt free.

"And I've done it. Four of them have graduated, and the fifth is doing very well. I'm absolutely delighted with them. The proudest days of my life have been spent watching them get their diplomas," Sandra said.

Money may seem like the clincher, here. But really, Sandra most wanted to give her loved ones joy in their work—a joy for which a college education prepares them. While still alive, she gave her offspring the gift of education, preparing them for careers of their choosing, and likely saving them from lives spent in low-paying, unfulfilling jobs. Since all gifts were paid in direct reimbursement of tuition bills, none were taxed by the federal government.

• Give a gift that will grow in value. Lucky enough to have bought some stocks that just keep growing? The federal government can not tax future worth. So you may decide to give stocks to a loved one. You bought the stock six months ago, at a price of $3,000. They are now worth $9,000—$1,000 under the Unified Estate and Gift Tax credit. Give them away now. The government can't tax them—even if the stocks you bought six months back will, a year from now, be worth $15,000.

You may also give large gifts to your spouse without affecting your estate-tax credit. You may give, in a single calendar year:

• Any amount to your spouse, if he or she is a U.S. citizen.

• A gift of up to $100,000 per year if your spouse holds citizenship in a country other than the United States.

State Death Taxes

Certain states and one jurisdiction—Massachusetts, New York, Ohio, Oklahoma, and Puerto Rico—levy taxes against your estate. However, the federal government will credit your estate for any taxes it pays to these jurisdictions—so the overall tax levy on your estate does not increase because of these state taxes.

Inheritance Taxes

Certain states levy taxes against the value of the goods your loved ones receive from your estate. These states are the following: Connecticut, Delaware, Indiana, Iowa, Kansas, Kentucky, Loui-

SMART DEFINITION

Estate tax
Death tax

A tax levied against the wealth you leave behind.

Inheritance tax

A tax levied against the people who benefit from your estate.

Trusts

A system through which you can control, and benefit from, your assets, but not technically "own" them. Certain trusts can help minimize your tax levy.

F.Y.I.

Taxes are only imposed on the amount you leave in excess of estate-tax credits. If you die in 2010, leaving an estate of $1.8 million, and the estate-tax credit is $1 million, only $800,000 is subject to federal tax.

Death and Inheritance Taxes, by State and Jurisdiction

State	Levies Death Taxes	Levies Inheritance Taxes	State	Levies Death Taxes	Levies Inheritance Taxes
Alabama			Montana		*
Alaska			Nebraska		*
Arizona			Nevada		
Arkansas			New Hampshire		*
California			New Jersey		*
Colorado			New Mexico		
Connecticut		*	New York	*	
Delaware		*	North Carolina		*
District of Columbia			North Dakota		
Florida			Ohio	*	
Georgia			Oklahoma	*	
Hawaii			Oregon		
Idaho			Pennsylvania		*
Illinois			Puerto Rico	*	
Indiana		*	Rhode Island		
Iowa		*	South Carolina		
Kansas		*	South Dakota		*
Kentucky		*	Tennessee		
Louisiana		*	Texas		
Maine			Utah		
Maryland		*	Vermont		
Massachusetts	*		Virginia		
Michigan			Washington		
Minnesota			West Virginia		
Mississippi			Wisconsin		
Missouri			Wyoming		

siana, Maryland, Montana, Nebraska, New Hampshire, New Jersey, North Carolina, Pennsylvania, and South Dakota.

This means that if your loved ones live in one of these states, they may be taxed on what they inherit from you.

Legal Tax Loopholes

You've learned how much you can leave in your estate before the government taxes it. You've learned the limitations on gift giving. And you've learned whether you live in a jurisdiction that taxes your estate, or your heirs' inheritances.

If you're lucky enough to have an estate totaling more than $650,000 now, or if you expect it to total more than $1 million by 2006, it's time to start exploring the legal means of dodging a tax levy that ranges from 37 to 55 percent.

Trusts—a legal tax dodge—are explored thoroughly in the next chapter.

For now, though, let's look at some other means of leaving more of your estate to the people you love, rather than to the government you live under.

Take Advantage of Marital Deductions

The federal government allows you to leave an unlimited amount of cash and property tax free to your spouse, as long as your spouse is a U.S. citizen.

F.Y.I.

If you ever do need to pay a gift tax— it is the giver, not the receiver, who foots the bill.

F.Y.I.

If you give while you're still alive, you'll get to actually see the joyous looks on the faces of your loved ones.

Marital deductions do not apply to citizens of countries other than the United States. If you married a British national, what can you do? A few things. First, your spouse, regardless of nationality, can benefit from estate-tax credits now in force. If you die in 2007, you can leave him your entire $1 million estate, and it won't be taxed. If you have more money than that, consider taking advantage of the tax-free $100,000 gifts that you can give him each year.

Leaving everything you have to a spouse, tax free, may sound like a sweet deal—but sometimes it's not.

Think of it this way: You and Betsey are both 37 years old. You die in a freak accident. Leaving your $2 million estate to her was probably a fine idea. Odds are, Betsey will have years and years ahead of her to figure out how to minimize the tax bill for her future heirs, taking advantage of new tax laws and tax shelters along the way.

However, say you and Betsey are both 87. You die, leaving her your entire $2 million estate. Betsey will probably not outlive you by very long. Your eventual heirs will be stuck with paying taxes on $1 million. (Assuming you die in 2006 or later.)

Older couples wondering how to best protect large estates from federal taxes are often best off using a Bypass Trust, which is discussed thoroughly in chapter 4.

Equalize Your Estates

If one spouse's personal estate far outweighs the other's, it can be a good idea to give your spouse some extra cash or property to bring your estate under the tax-exempt cap.

Help May Be on the Way

You should know, though, about some governmental initiatives that may help ease the burden.

In early 1999, U.S. Representatives John Tanner (Democrat from Tennessee) and Jennifer Dunn (Republican from Washington) joined forces to introduce a tax-relief bill that would eliminate estate taxes on farms and small businesses by 2011.

For more information, contact the following organizations. They all back the bill:

- American Farm Bureau: (847) 685-8600

- National Federation of Independent Businesses: (615) 872-5300

- U.S. Chamber of Commerce: (202) 659-6000

It works like this: The year is 2008. Jerry has an estate worth $1.3 million. His wife, Susie, has an estate worth $500,000. Only the first $1 million of any estate is exempt from federal taxes. They have each determined the value of their individual estates. They live in a community property state and have been able to delineate their individual estates, taking into account what assets each owned before the marriage and which assets acquired after marriage they are legally allowed to hold separately. (See chapter 2.) Since his wife is a U.S. citizen, Jerry knows he can give her an unlimited amount of money during any calendar year. He gives her $300,000. Now Jerry's estate totals $1 million; Susie's, $800,000. Neither estate will owe Uncle Sam a dime (both fall under the $1 million estate-tax credit cap of 2006).

F.Y.I.

Any amount you give over $10,000 ($20,000 per couple) to any single person during a single calendar year will be deducted from your federal estate-tax credit. You don't have the option of paying the tax at the time the gift is given. It must wait until your estate is settled. The only exception to this is if you give away, during your lifetime, an amount exceeding the federal estate-tax credit. If, by 2006, you have given away more than $1 million (the estate-credit cap for that year) you will have to pay taxes on your gifts by the end of the tax year.

This scenario works out fine, as long as Jerry has left his goods to loved ones other than his wife, Susie.

If, as usual, he has left all his goods to his wife, Susie's heirs may face a problem.

After Jerry's death, Susie controls an estate worth $1.8 million, $800,000 of which is, if left outright, subject to federal taxation.

In order to avoid exorbitant federal taxation, Jerry and Susie should employ trusts and other tax-avoidance tools discussed thoroughly in the next chapter.

Give It Away

You've learned that you can give, in any calendar year, $10,000 tax free to any individual, and without the feds deducting your gift from your estate-tax credit. Married persons can give $20,000 per year.

Understand that neither you nor the recipient will suffer any tax consequences as a result of these gifts.

If you are a person of significant means, this is a terrific way to avoid estate taxes. While you're still hale and hearty, give each of your 15 beloved nieces and nephews a $10,000 gift each year. If you're married, double it. You won't own the IRS a dime.

If you are a single person giving any one person, in a calendar year, more than $10,000; or a partner in a married couple giving more than $20,000, taxes must be paid to the IRS. It is always the giver, not the receiver, who pays taxes due.

But sometimes $10,000 or even $20,000 thousand just won't cut it. Your child loses his job and needs an emergency bridge loan. Your son and daughter-in-law have found a great deal on a starter home, and you really want to buy it for them.

What to do? Here are some ideas:

• **Remember the calendar-year rule.** You can only give, depending on your marital status, $10,000 or $20,000 to any individual during any calendar year. Remember though: December 31 marks the end of one year; January 1 the beginning of the next.

• **Give as a couple, to a couple.** If your daughter and son-in-law really want that starter home, and you want to give it to them, you and your husband can give your daughter $20,000 without fear of tax penalty. You and your husband can also give your son-in-law $20,000 without fear of tax penalty, effectively doubling the couple's buying power.

• **Give over time.** A loved one has expressed her desire to work five or six years in the corporate world, then start her own businesses. She expects start-up costs of $50,000. You can simply give her $10,000 a year over the next five years.

Credit for Foreign Death Taxes

If you own any property in a foreign country, and that country taxes your estate, your heirs can claim those levies as a credit against U.S. federal estate taxes.

STREET SMARTS

John S. is a 67-year-old widower living in central Florida. When his son's pickup truck showed signs of giving up the ghost, John decided to treat him to a new one.

John Jr. is an independent contractor. "He works up north, in a tri-state area," John S. said. "He needs reliable transportation, and I was in a position to help." The only problem: the pickups John Jr. looked at fell well beyond the $10,000 tax-free gift allowance. How did father and son get around this dilemma? John S. gave John Jr. $10,000 in December 1997 and $8,000 in January 1998. By the end of that month, John Jr. was happily driving around New York, New Jersey, and Connecticut in his new pickup. Dad's tax liability was zero.

Life Insurance

While life insurance payoffs are generally considered part of your estate, you can bypass any possible tax consequences for your heirs by putting them in trusts. This process is discussed thoroughly in the next chapter.

Special Cases

The $1 million estate-tax credit is a boon for most Americans. For others, especially people who inherit nonliquid assets, it just doesn't go far enough.

You have run your family farm your whole life. Your son has helped, his whole life. There was never any doubt that the land is to pass into his hands upon your death.

And it does. The only problem, though, is that your ten thousand acres in the Midwest are valued at $4 million. Your heir's tax rate? Even taking advantage of a $1 million estate-tax credit, he'll end up paying the federal government 55 percent of $3 million—or $1.65 million.

Your land may be worth a small fortune, but it's not as if your son is so rich that he has $1.65 million sitting around in a bank account. How does he raise the cash? Does he sell the farm?

Farmers aren't the only ones facing this problem. Your loved ones may encounter a similar scenario inheriting Dad's lumber yard, or Mom's horseback-riding academy.

Situations such as these demand special consideration, and you absolutely must speak with a qualified estate lawyer about how to minimize estate-tax levies for your heirs.

If You Have to Pay . . .

Reading this book, you'll learn how to minimize your estate-tax liability. However, your estate may still owe something to the federal government. You can use your will to make provisions for the distribution of taxes owed.

This is how it works:

Your executor will inventory all your assets, everything from your stocks to your home to your car. He deducts from this total all debts owing, including funeral expenses. He then takes into account all the tools you have used to avoid or postpone estate taxes (if you left all your money to your spouse via an unlimited marital deduction, for example). The result is your taxable estate. If it falls below the estate-tax credit for the year in which you die, terrific. If not, your estate will owe the federal government money, which your executor will pay to the IRS before distributing the remaining assets.

By now, you may wonder who should bear the brunt of your estate-tax levy. You have several options:

• **Ask that your taxes be paid "off the top."** Your lawyer can draft a will indicating your desire for estate taxes to be paid prior to the distribution of any goods, except those named in general bequests.

• **Mandate that each beneficiary pays his fair share.** If there are taxes to be paid from your estate, your will can require each beneficiary to pay a portion, based on the value of the goods you have bequeathed to that person.

SMART DEFINITION

General bequest

Any specific item that you will to a certain person. "I leave my beloved niece, Martha Jones, $5,000" is a general bequest; and so is, "I leave my beloved grandson, Mark Wright, my baseball-card collection."

Residuary estate

What is left over after taxes, debts, and general bequests have been paid out. The residuary estate is usually the largest segment of a will. For example, you may leave $5,000 to your niece, your baseball-card collection to your grandson, and your residuary estate to your wife. The residuary estate might include your house, $250,000 in savings, your car, and other valuables and in-valuables.

• **Pay taxes from a general bequest.** If you have left the lion's share of your estate to an individual or organization, you may think it appropriate for that individual or organization to pay the taxes on the full estate.

Some Final Sound Advice

David S. Rhine serves as national director of family wealth planning for the New York City accounting firm BDO Seidman in Manhattan. In an August 1998 interview with *Town & Country,* he outlined his views on tax-avoidance:

"Your first goal should be to make certain that your property goes to your chosen heirs," he said. "Your secondary goal should be to make sure that happens at the lowest tax cost."

There are a number of ways to legitimately minimize the taxes your estate will owe the federal government. You and your spouse may decide to equalize your estates. You may take advantage of the Unified Gift and Estate Tax credit to give away your goods during your lifetime. You may make use of certain trusts (which are discussed thoroughly in the next chapter). Still, before worrying about any of this, make sure that you've put in place an estate plan outlining which of your loved ones get which possessions.

THE BOTTOM LINE

The Unified Gift and Estate Tax allows Americans to leave, in 2006 and later, tax-free legacies of up to $1 million. The same tax code allows you to give another individual tax-free gifts of up to $10,000 per year. Leveling your estate and your spouse's estate may help your heirs avoid federal taxes on your legacy. If your spouse is a U.S. citizen, the goods you leave to him or her will not be subject to federal taxation upon your death, regardless of their worth. Certain states levy inheritance and death taxes against your legacy.

CHAPTER 4

....

Your Will

Wills are the most basic of estate-planning tools. They are legal documents delineating which of your loved ones get what part of your estate. Unfortunately, wills are virtually always subject to a long—and often costly—probate process.

Still, it's far better to die with a will serving as your only estate plan than it is to die intestate. If you die without a will or other estate plan, local governments will decide how to divvy up your assets. In general, under state intestacy laws, you can expect your spouse to get half of your assets and your kids to divide the other half. If you die without a spouse or children, expect your parents to get first claim on your goods, followed by your siblings and other relatives. If you die intestate, and without any identifiable heirs, your assets will revert to the state. And, if you die without a will naming personal and property guardians for your minor children, you forfeit your say in how they should be raised after your death.

Reading this book, you'll learn about a variety of trusts and other techniques that can help your heirs avoid the hassle of probate and, in many cases, save on estate taxes. Still, many estate planners believe that you only absolutely need three documents covering the end of your life and your wishes for your heirs. They are a will, a living will, and a durable power of attorney for health care. (You'll learn about the latter documents in chapter 8.)

You may not have the time, inclination, need, or cash to put your assets in trust. That's okay. But no one should die intestate.

Why You Need a Will

You may want to use a will as your primary estate planning tool or you may need to employ one as a backup to any other estate measures you've already established.

First, let's consider why you need a will—whatever your overall estate plan.

1. You need to take care of your kids. In most states, a will is the only estate-planning tool through which you can name personal and property guardians for your minor children. (You'll learn more about this in chapter 6.)

2. You need to back up your current estate plan. No matter how many different probate-avoidance tools you use, you will probably still need at least some basic will. This is why: You may die at a time when you've accrued significant assets but not had the opportunity to put them into your living trust. You may die while waiting for a loved one's will to go through probate—you expect to claim assets from this estate, but they're not technically yours until probate is established. A will in which you leave all your worldly possessions to your spouse, say, or equally divided between your spouse and children, will ensure that these possessions make their way into the hands of your loved ones.

In certain situations, despite the probate morass, a will can also legitimately serve as your primary estate-planning tool. Consider the following:

- **You're not dying any time soon.** If you are a young person with a seemingly limitless financial future, a will, for now, should probably serve as

F.Y.I.

No one should die intestate. This is doubly true for persons living in nontraditional households. Here's why:

Susan and Harry are a heterosexual married couple. Harry dies intestate. Most jurisdictions mandate that, as Harry's wife, Susan is entitled to part of his estate.

Now turn this scenario around. Harry and John have a long-term committed gay relationship. If Harry dies intestate, local laws will not automatically assume that John is entitled to anything. Why? The pair weren't legally "married." This same scenario holds true for heterosexual couples who have decided to cohabitat rather than marry. If you live in a nontraditional household and die intestate, those you love may receive nothing from your estate.

your primary estate-planning tool. Living trusts—discussed thoroughly in chapter 4—accomplish your estate goals while bypassing probate. Still, they take some money to start up, and if your financial picture is in a state of flux, you may spend a lot of money talking to lawyers who have to rewrite new trust documents every time you accrue a new asset. At this point in your life, it's simpler, and makes better financial sense, to write out a straightforward will, through which you can state something like, "I leave all my real and personal property to my wife, Jane Doe."

• **You can't deal.** Sure, you know you should examine trusts and other estate-planning tools, but you just don't have the time or the inclination. That's not a great approach (Trusts can save your heirs a lot of time and a lot of money, bypassing probate.) Still, it is better to die with a will as your sole estate plan than with no estate plan at all. If you die intestate, your government, working under state law, will determine who gets what. That's bad. You know your loved ones' needs far better than any government agency does.

• **Most of your assets won't be subject to probate, anyway.** Assets that you hold with another as joint tenants with the right of survivorship won't be subject to the probate process—they will simply pass to the other tenant upon your death. Similarly, life insurance policies won't pass through probate—the benefits will be paid out to your named beneficiaries. Other retirement and estate planning funds—such as Individual Retirement Accounts and retirement plans, also usually bypass probate by requiring that you name a beneficiary in the event of your death.

Legalities

A will is not a terribly complicated legal document. For example, here's the will of the late Warren Burger, former chief justice of the U.S. Supreme Court:

LAST WILL AND TESTAMENT OF WARREN E. BURGER

I hereby make and declare the following to be my last will and testament.

1. My executors will first pay all claims against my estate;
2. The remainder of my estate will be distributed as follows: one-third to my daughter, Margaret Elizabeth Burger Rose, and two-thirds to my son, Wade A. Burger;
3. I designate and appoint as executors of this will, Wade A. Burger and J. Michael Luttig.
IN WITNESS WHEREOF, I have hereunto set my hand to this my Last Will and Testament this 9th day of June, 1994.

Warren E. Burger

We hereby certify that in our presence on the date written above WARREN E. BURGER signed the foregoing instrument and declared it to be his Last Will and Testament and that at this request in his presence and in the presence of each other we have signed our names below as witnesses.

Nathaniel E. Brady
Alice M. Khu

F.Y.I.

Lots of people interpret the phrase "last will and testament" to mean "this is the last thing I'm doing before shuffling off this mortal coil." They're wrong. The word "last" in this case means "latest." That's important. Your latest will negates all previous documents.

Chief Justice Burger penned a very simple will. The will of American icon Elvis Presley is a bit more complicated. His will (reprinted in appendix A, pages 175–87) includes all of the clauses discussed in this chapter and also addresses the trusts he employed to take care of his daughter, Lisa Marie (then still a child), as well as other family members and assorted hangers-on. (More on trusts in chapters 5 and 7.)

Many people (even those of us who are not Supreme Court justices or swivel-hipped entertainers) think it best to hire a lawyer to draw up their wills, simply to make sure that all contingencies they want to cover are covered. Others feel comfortable drawing upon any one of the many do-it-yourself will kits available.

For your will to be legal:

• You must be at least 18 years old. If you live in Wyoming, you must be 19.

• You must be of sound mind.

• You must type out the document, or use a computer to print it out.

• You must name a beneficiary of your estate. (Even a single line such as "I leave all my possessions to my husband, John Smith" will do it.)

• You must name an executor.

• You must date the will.

• You must sign it in front of two witness who are not named as beneficiaries of the will. (If you live in Vermont, you need three witnesses.)

• Depending on your state, you may need to have the document notarized. If you work with a lawyer to draw up your will, she will tell you whether it needs to be notarized. If you buy a do-it-yourself will kit, it will indicate whether you need a public notary.

A will does not need to be filed in a courthouse until after your death. You should however, place a copy of it with the rest of your estate plans for easy access by your heirs. You should also give a copy to your executor and any close family members or friends who you want to know of your estate-planning decisions.

The Draft of the Will

Whether you're planning to buy a do-it-yourself will kit or to hire a lawyer to draw up the document for you, it never hurts to acquaint yourself with the overall "flow" of the document. (A sample will is supplied in appendix B, pages 189–93.)

The average will contains the following clauses and information:

• **The Introduction.** In this section, you identify yourself by name and address and indicate that this is your "last will and testament." You also state that you are of "sound mind." This is an important issue. Aggrieved would-be heirs will often challenge a will in court claiming that the writer—say, an 85-year old father who recently cut all his children out of his will to leave everything to his new, 23-year-old wife—was not of sound mind when signing the document. This is why all wills require

SMART SOURCES

If you want a do-it-yourself will, check out the variety of will kits available from Nolo press:

(800) 846-9455

www.nolo.com

witnesses. Your witnesses surely don't need to be trained psychiatrists, but the courts may call upon them to testify that your looked sane (at least to them) at the time you wrote your will.

The clause itself usually reads something like: "I, John Smith, of 123 Maple Street, Princeton, New Jersey, being of sound and disposing mind and memory, do make, publish, and declare this to be my Last Will and Testament, and I hereby revoke all wills and codicils heretofore made by me."

• **Personal Information.** This section states clearly what you mean by phrases like "my wife" and "my children." You want the courts to know that your use of the words "my wife" means your current wife, Catherine, not your ex-wife, Betty. You also want the judge to know whether the phrase "my children" includes your biological kids or your biological kids and stepchildren. Unlike children born in marriage, those born out of wedlock are not automatically assumed to inherit, so make sure you name them if you wish to leave them legacies.

The wording of this clause usually runs something like: "I am married to John X. Smith, and all references in this will to my husband are to him. I have three children, whose names and dates of birth are:

Susan Q. Smith, December 4, 1965

Mark L. Smith, November 19, 1972

Harold A. Smith, October 8, 1975

• **Debts and Taxes.** As discussed in chapter 3, you can mandate that taxes and debts be paid "off the top"; that is, from the entire estate, from the residuary estate, or even from an individual request. Your will should contain a paragraph or two outlining how debts and taxes levied against the estate should be paid. It usually reads: "I direct that my debts and expenses shall be paid from [my residuary estate/entire estate/my bequest to . . .]. I direct that my inheritance, estate, and succession taxes, including interest and penalties, payable by reason of my death, shall be paid from [my residuary estate/entire estate/my bequest to . . .]."

• **Your Legacy.** This is where you list who gets what. You may make specific bequests to whomever you like ("I leave $3,000 to my nephew, Sam Smith. I leave my engagement ring to my granddaughter, Margaret Smith.") You also note to whom—usually a spouse—you are leaving your residuary estate. (As discussed in chapter 3, the residuary estate—anything not mentioned as a general bequest—is usually the largest portion of your legacy.)

• **Care of Minor Children.** If you have minor children, you must appoint a property guardian to manage the goods you leave to them and a personal guardian to raise them. This is discussed thoroughly in chapter 7.

• **Name an Executor.** As noted above, an "executor" is the person named in a will who has the responsibility of carrying out the terms of the will. This includes collecting the estate's assets, paying its debts and taxes, and distributing remaining assets in accordance with your wishes.

• **Your Signature and the Signature of Witnesses.** Your signature indicates that you actually wrote the document purported as being your will. The signatures of witnesses, people known by you, is proof of this.

The Power of the Executor

Most executors don't make decisions on how your estate assets are to be distributed. They only make sure that those assets are handed out in accordance with your will. But, sometimes, when wills are not clearly written, an executor can wield great power.

You're the executor of your dad's will, and going through his possessions, you find a stack of old papers at the bottom of his trunk: pages and pages of jottings, literate jottings, but no more a novel than an acorn is an oak tree.

As an executor, you've been charged with carrying out the terms of your father's will. But that document either didn't mention this ream or was ambiguous as to his wishes for it.

Most executors would probably read through the pages and photocopy it for his brothers and sisters and maybe a few of his dad's best friends. They'd all read it and smile and say, "Hey! Dad was working on a novel." Then stick it in a drawer someplace.

That's most executors called upon to disburse most literary scribblings.

The executor in our story, though, is named Patrick Hemingway. His dad? Nobel Prize winner Ernest Hemingway. At the time of this writing, Simon and Schuster is touting its imminent publication of Hemingway's last "novel," *True at First Light.*

Recent news reports have stated that Hemingway's will was unclear as to what he wanted done with his unfinished manuscripts. Did he want them published? Burned? No one knows.

Patrick Hemingway, as his father's literary executor, has taken it upon himself to publish several of these "bottom of the trunk" type novels. But *True at First Light* has proven the most controversial.

Many literary scholars say the book—a narrative covering one of Hemingway's seemingly endless African sojourns—simply isn't any good. They doubt that Hemingway, the consummate perfectionist, would have wanted it published.

To back up their claim, they note that Hemingway was a best-selling author until his death, by suicide, in 1961. Had he wanted to publish it, they say, he certainly could have.

Very few executors sit in Patrick Hemingway's position: trying to decide the final wishes of a literary giant. But when you write your will, make sure it clearly outlines how you want your property disbursed. And make sure that your executor knows your wishes, and will follow them, should confusion arise.

When It's Time to Change Your Will

Many people rewrite their wills several times over the course of their lives. Some examples of when you'll want to change your will:

WHAT MATTERS, WHAT DOESN'T

What Matters
• Taking the time now to draw up your will.

• Knowing that in certain situations a will alone is a perfectly sound estate-planning tool.

What Doesn't
• Worrying about the costs of probate if you've determined that a will is all you need.

• As new beneficiaries come into your life; the most common example is the birth of a new child.

• When beneficiaries—such as spouses—die.

• If you divorce.

• If the persons you have named as executor, personal guardian for your children, and person in whom you've placed a durable power of attorney for health chare or finances die or find themselves unable to serve.

You will also want to change your will as you acquire new assets and rid yourself of others. For example, you don't want to leave your home at 123 Maple Street to your beneficiaries if you've since moved and no longer own the house!

A legal document called a codicil can amend your current will. However, it is often simpler just to write an entirely new will. Codicils can be tricky and can lead to contests of your will in court.

Look at it this way: Suppose you wrote a will leaving your beloved nephew $25,000. Then the kid goes bad—he begins stealing, starts using cocaine, and generally gets into all types of trouble.

Wills are matters of public record. Therefore, when you die, your nephew can view your original will, view the codicil, see he's been cut out, and decide to challenge the will in court.

Had you simply written a new will, your nephew need not have known that you had planned to leave him anything in the first place—making the prospect of a challenge much less likely.

A Will or a Trust?

Do you want everybody to know what you're leaving and to whom? Wills are matters of public record.

When Frank Sinatra died in mid-1998, lots of newspapers gleefully reported which of the multi-millionaire's heirs was getting what.

The document guaranteed his current wife, Barbara Marx Sinatra, $3.5 million; his ex-wife, $250,000; and his kids, $200,000 each to supplement the trust funds he had established for them years earlier.

Barbara Marx Sinatra also inherited the entertainer's Rolls Royce, his three homes, and, probably most valuable, the right to market Ol' Blue Eyes's image and likeness. She can also count on the silverware and paintings.

Frank's son, meanwhile, got the crooner's collection of sheet music.

But don't think that the legacies noted in the entertainer's will encompassed all his wealth. All newspaper reports of the time stated that the will covered only a portion of Sinatra's assets. The rest had been placed in trusts.

We'll never know how Sinatra chose to distribute all his assets. Trusts are not matters of public record. Lots of people just don't care if anyone knows what they're leaving to their heirs. But if you do care, and you want your legacy to remain private, consider placing it in a trust.

In every venue, wills are matters of public record. Anyone can view them.

Probate, and Why It's a Pain

Probate is the process through which a will is "approved" and determined valid. During the probate process, lawyers and judges will identify the property in your estate, settle any debts levied against it, and dole out whatever is left to your beneficiaries.

How does probate work?

After you die, your executor—virtually always

F.Y.I.

The Estate Planning Information Center notes that probates take an average of nine months to two years. During that period, your loved ones have little to no access to your assets.

WARNING: PROBATE AHEAD

Probate delays the disbursement of assets. Sometimes that's annoying. Other times, it's devastating.

Wanda M. is a 44-year-old part-time receptionist. Her husband, in his will, left her everything he owned. She had always assumed that should her husband die unexpectedly, she and the children would be taken care of.

Graham did die unexpectedly. And Wanda was shocked to learn that his assets were frozen until probate was established. The process took more than a year.

"My job didn't pay enough for me and the kids to live on," Wanda recalls. "The two eldest had to move in with my sister and her husband and change their school. By the time it was all over, my son's original school wasn't satisfied with his year away and made him repeat a grade."

Wanda and her two younger children barely got by. As she and her lawyer waded through probate, they petitioned the judge to award a family allowance from the estate. They got it, but it totaled only a few hundred dollars.

If Wanda and Graham had placed their assets in a living trust, or held their bank accounts, home, and car as joint tenants with the right-of-survivorship, his legacy would have bypassed probate and put his worldly goods directly in her hands immediately—just when she needed them.

F.Y.I.

Depending on the venue in which you live the court handling probate is called a probate, surrogate, or chancery court.

working in tandem with a lawyer—will file your will in the probate court of the county in which you live; inventory your assets and your debts; and send a formal notice to each of your heirs saying that the will has been filed for probate. If any of your heirs wants to contest the will, he will do so now. If no one questions your provisions, a probate judge will approve the will. Your executor then pays any debts owed by your estate (including estate taxes) and disperses remaining assets to your beneficiaries.

Your executor will almost certainly have to hire a probate lawyer to file your will and to represent your estate through this process. (Some states won't even allow the executor to file the papers on his own.) Probate lawyers traditionally charge a fee based on the overall value of your estate.

Probate, then, virtually demands that some of the cash in your estate goes not to your loved ones, but to lawyers. Second, the entire process—from filing your will to disbursing assets to your heirs–often takes months, and can, in some cases, take years. While interim payments can occasionally be made to your heirs before probate is established, in general, your heirs will have to wait for the process to run itself out before they can get control of your assets. And you probably want your heirs to take control of their legacies earlier, rather than later.

Finally, probate can inconvenience your heirs, and put them through psychological distress.

• **Inconvenience:** Since probate takes place in the venue in which you die, it may prove inconvenient for your executors—especially if you have moved late in life, and your executor, say a daughter, now lives thousands of miles away. In addition, probate may have to be established in any venue in which you own property. Say you live in New York but have a vacation ranch in New Mexico. Your executor may have to file your will in these two venues and wait for two entirely separate courts to approve your will before disbursing assets to your beneficiaries.

• **Psychological implications:** It may be harder for your loved ones to get over your death and get on with their lives if they have to wait forever for the last business of your life—that is, probate, and the disbursement of your estate.

Why You Should Bother Reading the Rest of This Book

Wills are the most common—and in some cases, the only necessary—estate-planning tool. You have told the government how you want the assets divided in the event of your death.

That's fine.

However, other estate-planning tools can accomplish this same goal, saving your heirs probate time and expense, and, in some cases, minimize the tax levy on your legacy.

These techniques include trusts and owning property as "joint tenants with the right of survivorship."

Trusts and their benefits are examined thoroughly in the next chapter.

You learned about joint tenancy with the right of survivorship in chapter 2. It is a legal means through which two or more persons (spouses, say, or parent and child, or other life partners) hold title to an asset (such as a home). When one tenant dies, the other tenants automatically take possession of his share. Holding an asset as joint tenants with the right of survivorship bypasses probate.

THE BOTTOM LINE

If you have neither the time, cash, nor inclination to develop a full-fledged estate plan, at least take the time to write up a will. If you don't, you give your government the power to decide which of your loved ones receives what assets from your estate.

Wills also back up your other estate plans. However, for the smoothest possible transition of assets from your estate to the hands of your loved ones, consider trusts and other probate-avoidance tools.

CHAPTER 5

....

Put Your Trust in Trusts

Trusts are legal systems through which you or someone you love benefit from your assets but don't technically own them. Like some corporations, trusts are paper entities that have the ability to own property.

When you place your assets in trusts, you no longer actually own them. The trust that you've assigned does.

Think about it this way: You have a neighbor, a small-business owner named John Jones. Mr. Jones drives a 1999 Honda Accord. You assume it's his car. But your wrong. The car technically belongs to his company, John Jones Inc. For whatever reason (probably for tax purposes), Mr. Jones decided that it made more sense for his company to own the car than for him, personally, to do so.

This doesn't mean that Mr. Jones can't drive the car. You see him riding around all the time. He takes it to and from work and business appointments. He uses it to drop the kids off at soccer practice and to take his wife to their favorite restaurant on their "date nights." He just doesn't, technically, own it.

Trusts, depending on which ones you choose, can operate in much the same way. Let's say you own a home, and, for various reasons discussed later in this chapter, you decide to place it in trust. You meet with a lawyer. He draws up the trust documents. You sign over the deed to your house from "Michael and Paula Brown" to the "Michael and Paula Brown Living Trust." You still live in the house. You still decide how to decorate it. You still mow the lawn each Sunday. Assuming you've appointed yourself and your spouse as a trustees—that is, the people in charge of administering the trust—you can even sell the place when you feel like it. It just technically does not belong to you anymore—it belongs to the trust.

You'll learn a lot in this chapter about using trusts to avoid taxes and otherwise protect and distribute your assets.

What Exactly Is a Trust?

More than just these financial arrangements that all those wealthy kids have in college, trusts are legal systems through which you or someone you love benefit from your assets but don't technically own them. Trusts often serve as sound estate-planning tools. They can help reduce your estate-tax levy. And, since they bypass probate, they make for an easy transfer of assets from you to your heirs. Charitable trusts can even help lower your income tax payments.

Trusts fall into one of two broad categories: revocable and irrevocable. Any revocable trust you establish can be changed or rescinded during your lifetime. An irrevocable trust—such as the life-insurance trust discussed below—can not be altered once you have put it in place.

Why would you want to revoke a trust?

Lots of reasons. Life situations change often. You may set up an A/B trust to benefit your spouse after your death. But what if you divorce? You'd clearly want to revoke that trust.

In fact, you'd probably like the ability to change your mind as often as you like, and revoke any trust you implement. But, as noted above, some trusts—notably life-insurance trusts and

SMART DEFINITION

Revocable trust

One that can be changed or rescinded during your lifetime. An irrevocable trust can not be altered once you have put it in place.

F.Y.I.

An A/B trust is also called a credit shelter trust, exemption trust, or marital life estate trust.

The IRS will allow a surviving spouse to use A/B trust principal. However, you can write your trust to specifically forbid the life beneficiary from having access to those funds—thereby ensuring that your final beneficiaries, say your children, enjoy a share in your estate.

SMART DEFINITION

Document of trust

A legal document that, once signed, creates a trust.

charitable trusts—have been deemed irrevocable by federal and local governments. Why? They provide substantial tax breaks for their beneficiaries. Governments don't want you taking advantage of these tax savings then saying, "No no no, I changed my mind, and I'm revoking the trust."

Since you can't alter irrevocable trusts once they have been put in force, you want to talk to an estate lawyer about the ramifications of putting your assets in such a vehicle.

Store all your trust documents in the "estate box" discussed in chapter 2.

A/B Trusts

An A/B trust is a system through which two persons—usually married—put their individual estates in trust for the other. Many married couples employ these trusts in order to save their eventual heirs—usually, their children—estate taxes.

A/Bs effectively save traditional families from the drudgery of double taxation. Without them, you run the risk of your children's overall legacy being taxed twice, once upon the death of your spouse, and then again upon your death.

How an A/B Trust Works

Let's take a look at how an A/B trust works.

First, the letters:

The letters "A/B" in the A/B trust designate the trust of the first spouse to die (the "A" trust) and that of the surviving spouse (the "B" trust.) Only the "A" trust ever becomes active. The spouses have left their estates in trust for each other. After one spouse dies, there is no one left for the "B" trust to benefit.

The person instituting the trust and his or her spouse sign A/B trust documents, setting up trusts which do not become operational until one of them dies. Typically, each partner will name the other as the life beneficiary, and name other heirs (usually children) as final beneficiaries.

This is not a hard-and-fast rule, however. If one spouse has no aptitude for dealing with money, he or she may mutually decide to appoint an outside trustee—a close friend or relative, a bank or a trust company—to manage trust assets. (You'll find more information on choosing a trustee later in this chapter.)

When one partner dies, his trust goes to the surviving spouse. Any estate taxes due are paid. The survivor receives income generated by the trust, and can use the principal, the IRS says, "for health, education, support, and maintenance in his or her accustomed manner of living."

However, the spouse doesn't actually own the trust, so when he dies, the trust's property passes tax free to its final beneficiaries, usually the couple's children.

When the second spouse dies, her final beneficiaries inherit the property in the trust (the "B" trust) and your final beneficiaries inherit the property in your trust. Remember, the property held in your "A" trust will not be taxed again, because your spouse only "benefited" from that property, she did not technically "own" it. And also, because your spouse never "owned" the assets in your trust, she cannot will them away at her death. You have decided who the final beneficiaries of the "A" trust are.

SMART SOURCES

As with any entity controlling property or funds, you'll find that trusts require some IRS paperwork. Trustees must contact the IRS to receive a taxpayer identification number for the trust, and fill out a trust-income tax return each year. You can download the appropriate form, 1041, from the service's web site:

www.irs.gov

Any applicable estate taxes will be charged against your "A" trust at the time of the first spouse's death. Therefore, A/B trusts are often used in tandem with a marital deduction to minimize tax levies.

Say you die in 2010, when the estate-tax cap is $1 million. You leave behind a $2 million estate. A specific "formula clause" in your trust document can mandate that the trust hold only an amount of money/property that falls under the estate-credit tax cap at the time of your death. You can leave the rest of your property to your spouse, taking advantage of the unlimited "marital deduction" discussed in chapter 3. In the scenario above, the first spouse to die would leave a trust of $1 million, and the rest to his wife as a nontaxable "marital deduction." The total tax levy on your $2 million estate? Nothing.

Take a look at how an A/B trust might pan out in real life.

In 1999, Harry and Sally are both 72 years old. Together, they own $1.9 million in assets. They equalize their estates, so that each totals $950,000, and set up an A/B trust, a trust with a formula clause saying that only the amount of money that is exempt from federal taxation may be left in the trust. The rest goes outright to the spouse as a marital deduction.

Harry dies in 2008, when the estate-tax credit cap is $1 million. He has left only $950,000 in his estate, so no taxes are owed. Through the use of the A/B trust, Sally continues to benefit from Harry's assets until her death in 2010. Her estate, also worth $950,000, falls below the $1 million estate-tax credit for that year. So her heirs, her children, inherit her assets tax free. Since Harry named their children as his final beneficiaries, they also inherit the assets in his $950,000 trust, and they inherit tax free.

Had Harry and Sally simply left their assets to each other outright, their estate, at the time of Sally's death, would have totaled $1.9 million. The federal government would have taxed $900,000 of that, to their children's detriment.

Or consider another scenario involving a couple and their child:

John and Mary are married and they have one daughter, Hannah. John and Mary set up an A/B trust, naming each other as life beneficiaries and Hannah as their final beneficiary.

When John dies, his estate pays any applicable taxes on assets over the estate-credit tax cap for that year. His trust then takes effect. Mary, his life beneficiary, benefits from the income generated by the trust and can even use the principal in certain cases. However, since she does not technically own the property—she only *benefits* from the trust—they do not become part of her estate.

When Mary dies, the trust terminates. Hannah receives the assets in John's trust tax free. She may have to pay taxes on Mary's estate, but not on John and Mary's combined marital assets.

A/Bs are revocable trusts.

Bypass Trusts

As noted above, A/B trusts are for married couples. Single people, though, have their own legal means of putting their assets in trust for another. These are called "bypass trusts." Single people employ these trusts to ensure the financial support of loved ones during their lives and to save their even-

SMART MONEY

You learned in chapter 3 about the tax consequences of leaving legacies that total more than $650,000 now, or $1 million by 2006. Tax levies on such estates run from 37 to 55 percent. That's why many estate professionals strongly believe in the use of trusts to shelter some of your assets.

David S. Rhine, a family-wealth executive with BOD Seidman accounting firm in New York City, said in a recent issue of *Money* magazine, "At these rates, it's very possible that much of the wealth you've accumulated over your entire life won't make it to your kids."

Trusts can help minimize these exorbitant estate-tax levies.

tual heirs estate taxes. Bypass trusts are also revocable trusts.

They work like this.

Bypass Trusts for Life Partners

Tony and Mark are an unmarried couple. They have a combined estate of $1.4 million—with Mark owning $500,000 in property and cash; Tony, $900,000 in property and cash. Each partner wants to ensure the continued support of the other in the event of one partner's death.

Say Tony dies in 2003, when the estate credit is $700,000. If he decides to leave his estate to Mark outright, the federal government will tax the excess—$200,0000.

However, the couple can level their estate through the use of a bypass trust, with Tony and Mark each "owning" $700,000. When Tony dies, Mark can make use of the trust for the rest of his life, and the remainder, or principal (depending on stipulations noted in trust documents) will go to Tony's final beneficiaries upon Mark's death.

Bypass Trusts for Other Loved Ones

Single persons will sometimes use bypass trusts if they worry that combining their modest estate with the modest estate of a loved one will form a fortune that surpasses the estate-tax credit.

Think of it this way. You are an 83-year-old single woman with an estate of about $500,000. You die in 2010, when the estate-tax credit is $1 million. You leave your total estate to your 80-year-old brother, who, you know, will eventually leave it to his children.

No problem, you think. Your estate won't be taxed. And it won't be, during the first death go-round.

But consider this: Your 80-year-old brother won't outlive you by terribly long. He'll leave all his money to his kids—both his own $800,000 legacy and your $500,000.

When your brother dies, your beloved niece and nephew will be stuck paying federal taxes on $300,000. Why? The estate-tax credit is only $1 million, and your brother has left them a total of $1.3 million.

If you use a bypass trust, naming your brother as its life beneficiary, and your niece and nephew as its final beneficiaries, the kids won't have to pay any money to the federal government. No estate taxes will be owed on your trust when you die—it falls under the cap. Your brother only benefits from your trust, he doesn't own it—so, at his death, your trust isn't considered part of his estate. The kids get $1.3 million tax free.

Living Trusts

A living trust is often used as a "will replacement" and allows for the quick transfer of your property in case of your death or incompetence.

You meet with a lawyer to set up a trust and transfer your assets into it. As discussed above, if you're placing your home in trust, for example,

F.Y.I.

If you're a privacy hound, consider this: Wills are usually a matter of public record, which means that anyone who wants to know what you left at death, and what you gave to whom, can hop over to the courthouse and learn all about it. Trusts, however, are generally not considered public information. Nobody but the principals involved will know anything about your legacy.

you sign over the deed from "John Doe" to the "John Doe Living Trust." You can transfer as much or as little property as you like. You serve as the trustee. In that capacity, you can make the same investment-and-use decisions about your assets that you always have. There are no restrictions on your use of your assets.

But you also name a successor trustee to take over in the event of your death or incompetence. In the case of married couples, the successor trustee is most often a spouse. You also name a final beneficiary—again, in the case of married couples, usually a child.

If you die or become incapacitated, the property in the trust is automatically transferred to the management of your successor trustee. This process allows for another person's quick access to cash and property, if needed—if you die or become incapacitated. It also bypasses probate.

Living trusts can be either revocable or nonrevocable.

Generation-Skipping Transfer Trust

Some well-to-do couples may consider leaving up to $2 million, tax free, to their grandchildren through the use of a generation-skipping transfer trust.

This is how it works:

You set up a trust for persons in your family at least two generations removed from you—that is, the grandkids. In that trust an individual may place $1 million; a married couple, $2 million. The trust assets become your grandchildren's, tax free, at an age you specify.

Some couples consider employing this type of trust to avoid their grandchildren's legacy being taxed twice—first upon their death and then upon the death of their children, the grandkids parents.

Think of it this way: Mark and June have a son named Bob and two granddaughters, Annie and Susan. Mark and June die with a $5 million estate. They leave it to Bob outright. The estate is taxed. Bob combines the remainder with his own assets.

When Bob dies, his legacy—including both his assets and the goods inherited from his parents—goes, again outright, to Annie and Susan.

Since, even after taxes paid on their grandparents' estate, that legacy still exceeds the federal-tax credit cap, it will, in effect, be taxed again as Annie and Susan take control of their dad's inheritance.

Had Mark and June employed a generation-skipping trust, Annie and Susan could have enjoyed a $2 million legacy from their grandparents, tax free.

There's an important caveat to this tax dodge, however. If your generation-skipping trust totals more than $1 million, or more than $2 million for couples, your grandkids will be hit with a generation-skipping transfer tax totaling 55 percent. This is in addition to any other taxes owed on your estate. The government has put this rule into effect to keep wealthy families from skirting taxes altogether by simply bypassing their children and leaving all their wealth to their grandchildren.

F.Y.I.

If you transfer an already existing policy into a trust, and you die within three years, the benefits paid out by that policy will be taxed if they bring your total estate over the estate-credit cap. A life-insurance trust that is created before the actual purchase of the policy contains no such "you better outlive it by three years" rule. That's why this section strongly suggests buying new insurance. Talk to a qualified lawyer.

Irrevocable Life-Insurance Trust

If you're afraid that the value of your life insurance combined with your other assets will subject your estate to federal tax, you may want to consider a life-insurance trust. Always irrevocable, these are a legal means through which the benefits paid out by your life-insurance company pass directly to your heirs without being taxed. Because you've put your policy in trust, the payout is not considered part of your estate, so there are no taxes on them.

They work this way:

• Your lawyer drafts a nonrevocable life-insurance trust. You name a trustee and your beneficiaries. You then go shopping for a life-insurance policy. You find one you like. (For more information on how to shop for life insurance, see chapter 6.) You and your insurance counselor figure out the cost of the first premium. For legal reasons, you don't buy the policy yet. Instead, you place an amount of money equal to what your first premium will cost in your irrevocable life-insurance trust.

• Your trustee sends a written notice to your heirs stating that they have been named as beneficiaries of the trust. The notice also states that they have a given period of time—most often 30 days—to withdraw their share of the money you have deposited in the trust. Your beneficiaries should understand, well before receiving this notice, that it is to their benefit to receive their funds from your life-insurance policy payout rather than to withdraw a little cash now.

• Once the 30 days has passed—and none of your beneficiaries have made a claim against your trust—the trustee uses the cash gift you made to the trust to buy a life-insurance plan.

• You continue to make cash gifts to the trust equal to the cost of your life-insurance premiums. The trustee uses this money to pay for the premiums.

• At your death, your life-insurance benefits are paid out to your beneficiaries. These benefits are not considered part of your estate and are therefore not taxed.

Charitable Trusts

Charitable trusts do more than help the homeless, or the arts, or wildlife. They can help you, too, by reducing your federal income-tax rate and eventual estate taxes.

They differ from other trusts discussed here because they also provide you some cash benefits while you're still alive to enjoy them.

Charitable trusts are irrevocable.

Here's some information on the three types of charitable trusts: Pooled Income Trusts, Charitable Remainder Trusts, and Charitable Lead Trusts.

Pooled Income Trust

Consider a pooled income trust to be a mutual fund for a good cause. It allows persons of modest means to contribute to charitable organizations in

F.Y.I.

Your pooled income trust may demand an initial investment of $5,000 to $10,000. But what if you like how the trust is performing, would like to invest more, but can't come up with another five grand right now? Have no fear. Many of these trusts allow you to increase your contribution in increments of as little as $1,000.

Note, though, that pooled income trusts accept cash only. You can not contribute real or personal property to them.

an estate-planning-friendly way. You reap tax savings, and receive monetary dividends. And you don't need the big bucks necessary to establish a charitable trust of your own.

It works like this:

A charity sets up its own pooled income trust, and accepts contributions from individual investors. The trust will probably demand an initial minimum investment of between $5,000 to $10,000.

You make that contribution and deduct it, as allowed, from your federal income taxes.

The pooled income trust, meanwhile, invests the contributions made by its members. It pays dividends to its members if its investments prove profitable. It continues to pay you dividends for the rest of your life.

When you die, the principal contribution goes to the charity. Depending on the amount of your remaining estate, this contribution, like all other charitable contributions, can significantly help reduce your taxes, in this case, on the value of your estate.

Charitable Remainder Trust

Usually employed by people who have at least $100,000 to give, a "charitable remainder" is an irrevocable trust. It allows you to give property—cash, stocks, bonds, real estate, and other assets—to a good cause. The charity manages the trust and distributes at least part of the income generated from it to you or someone else you name. This income includes interest, stock profits, or any other money generated by the trust. Say you give the trust a rental property. The rents received by the trust would be considered trust income. After a certain period of time—either a number of years specified by you or after you or your beneficiaries die—the charity receives the property outright.

Charitable Lead Trust

A charitable lead trust is an estate-tax savings tool used by the very wealthy. You transfer significant cash, cash equivalents, or property to a charitable trust. You pay estate taxes at the time of transfer. The trust pays the charity a portion of its assets for a specified number of years. Eventually, the balance of the assets in the trust revert to your beneficiaries—with little or no additional federal estate taxes owed. This works particularly well with assets that are likely to appreciate in value over the years.

Other Trust Options

Thus far in this chapter, you've learned about some of the most common types of trusts. There are, however, a plethora of trusts available—all of which can help you better plan your estate to the benefit of your heirs. Talk to a qualified estate planner or estate lawyer. Here's a very brief overview of some other types of trusts you may encounter:

Disclaimer Credit-Shelter Trust Will

This will/trust hybrid allows the heirs named in your will to disclaim any property you may leave to them, instead putting the property in trust for another person.

Let's assume you're a single woman, and your will outlines your intent to leave your entire estate to your closest friend. Under the terms of your will, if your best friend should die before you, your estate goes to her children.

You die first and your friend is independently wealthy. She doesn't want or need your assets. Worse, she fears that your assets, combined with hers, will mean a heavy estate-tax levy for her kids one day.

A disclaimer credit-shelter trust will allows your friend to disclaim any rights to your assets, which are then placed in a trust for her children.

General Power of Appointment Trust

This is a marital trust allowing you to place certain limitations on the distribution of the assets you leave to your spouse. While your spouse must receive all the income from the trust, you take steps to protect the principal.

Let's say your spouse is a poor money manager, and you don't want him handling or investing the principle of your trust—fearing that there will be nothing left for your children after his death. You can stipulate, in a general power of appointment trust, that your spouse is entitled to trust income only, and appoint another trustee to handle and preserve the principal.

Qualified Terminable Interest (QTIP) Trust

A marital trust, the qualified terminable interest trust postpones the payment of estate taxes until the second spouse dies, and usually places strict limitations on the surviving spouse's use of the trust principal. This type of trust is often used by affluent couples who have children from prior marriages, and want to ensure that those children receive a legacy at the death of the second spouse. These trusts are often complicated to establish, and anyone considering the use of a QTIP should speak with a qualified lawyer.

Choosing a Trustee

Any trust requires four executives: the person setting up the trust, the life beneficiary, the final beneficiary, and the trustee.

Some of these roles may be played by the same person. For example, you may set up a living trust—one in which you are both trustee and life beneficiary.

You're probably not worried about who to appoint as your life beneficiary or even your final beneficiary. Most people don't say, "I should set up a trust, but I don't really know whom the trust should benefit." Instead, they think, "I want to be sure that I take care of my wife and my kids. What type of trust will serve them best?"

The appointment of a trustee, however, can prove a tricky matter.

Let's face it. In many of the trusts discussed above—an A/B trust for example, or a living trust—your spouse is likely to be your life beneficiary, and is also a perfectly fine choice as trustee.

But not always. Maybe your husband has never balanced a checkbook in his life and would prove incapable of managing $2 million in assets. Maybe your wife is disabled, and the management of those assets would prove too stressful. Maybe you're afraid that your current spouse will use up not only the trust income but its principal, and your final beneficiaries—such as children from a previous marriage—will be left with nothing.

In these cases, whom should you appoint as trustee?

Your choices are either institutional or personal—that is, you can appoint a trust company, bank trust department, or a trusted friend or relative. You can even appoint a beneficiary as trustee.

Let's take a look at the pros and cons of each option.

Choosing a Friend, Relative, or Someone Known to the Family

You may decide to set up a trust that requires your beneficiaries to ask the trustee for permission for extraordinary expenditures. A friend or relative will likely have more insight than a bank trust department into the needs of your loved ones. Your best friend will more carefully weigh your beneficiaries' needs in determining whether the trust can afford the requested expenditure.

However, your best friend's love for your beneficiaries may lead to his becoming caught in family crossfire, because your various beneficiaries may have different ideas about how trust assets should be spent.

Consider the following scenario:

Your son, a carpenter, has found a great deal on a house and would like $20,000 for a down payment.

Your daughter, an investment banker, wants that cash to remain in the trust, to be invested and reinvested.

Should your trustee give your son $20,000 for a house down payment, as he wants, or reinvest that cash, as your daughter would prefer? A trustee who has a personal relationship with your family may find this a hard decision to make—he won't want to endanger his relationship with either of your offspring.

Also, in appointing a close friend or relative as trustee, you have to consider whether she has the savvy to continue investing and reinvesting trust assets. If not, she may have to call in financial planners and others for help managing the trust, and those professional fees can add up.

Choosing Your Beneficiary As Trustee

With the exception of your spouse, it is often a bad idea to appoint a beneficiary as trustee. Too many conflicts of interest can arise.

Suppose you have created an A/B trust, naming your wife as life beneficiary and your daughter as both trustee and final beneficiary. Your wife wants to take a $10,000 European vacation. She asks your daughter to sign off on this extraordinary expenditure. When determining whether to allow this expenditure, will your daughter truly look at whether the trust can afford it, or will she think, "If Mom doesn't take this vacation, that's $10,000 more I inherit when she dies"?

Your daughter may be an upright and decent person, but human nature dictates that she will sometimes view her mother's expenditures as debits against her own eventual inheritance.

Choosing an Institutional Trustee

You may decide to name trust companies or bank trust departments as your trustees. Clearly, the professional money managers employed by these institutions are best equipped to make dispassionate choices. They will dole out and invest your cash as prudence dictates. However, they may turn a blind eye to the human enrichment money can bring.

Your son, a burgeoning photographer, may have an opportunity to take a $7,000 photo safari. The bank may think this a foolish expenditure. Had you still been alive, you may have thought that the opportunity for your son to photograph giraffes in the wild was well worth the dough. A friend or relative named as trustee, one who truly knows your son, may also have approved the cash for this trip.

Clearly, the appointment of a trustee can be a tricky decision. One way to ensure that your trust is managed smoothly after your death is to sit down now with your beneficiaries and ask them whom they would like to see in the role. Listen to their input, then make your own decision.

For information on special trust situations, such as continuing care for disabled loved ones, see chapter 8.

THE BOTTOM LINE

A/B trusts, bypass trusts, life-insurance trusts and generation-skipping transfer trusts can all help minimize the tax levy on your legacy. Charitable trusts help shelter your assets and also provide you with cash dividends while you're still alive to enjoy them. Living trusts provide easy transfer of wealth in the event of your death or illness. Speak with a qualified lawyer before putting any valuables in an irrevocable trust. The choice of a trustee can be a tricky business. Frank discussions with your heirs regarding who should serve in this role can help minimize family money squab-bles after your death.

Life Insurance Is for the Living

When you were a kid, you rejoiced in June and dreaded Labor Day. Why? You knew the school bell rang shortly after that long weekend. So around mid-August you seriously started jamming your days with as much fun as possible. If you hadn't spent enough time wading in the creek, you made sure to take a few extra trips down. If your tree house still lacked a door, you got out the hammer and nails. You knew when the summer would end, and you knew when you didn't have much time left.

Life is nothing like that. You never know when the bell will ring. A 75-year-old woman with leukemia may go into remission and live for another decade. Meanwhile, her perfectly healthy 35-year-old neighbor might be killed by a drunk driver while making his way home from work one evening.

If others depend on your earning power for their financial support, you must buy life insurance. You're never, ever, too young, or too healthy, to be "bothered" with this purchase.

Life Insurance: The Basics

Deciding which life insurance policy to buy is generally considered to be not quite as much fun as a good, long, root canal. The policy types themselves are likely to engender fear in the consumer. What is "level term" insurance? What does "cash value" mean?

If you're feeling a little stupid, take heart. An

old adage, "Life insurance is sold, not bought," should indicate that you are not alone in your confusion.

Later in this chapter, we will examine the types of life-insurance policies. You'll learn how to determine which will best serve your needs.

For now, though, remember this: your primary objective in buying life insurance is to ensure the continued financial support of your loved ones in the event of your death.

Let's consider why, and whether, you actually need it.

Who Needs It?

In general, you only need life insurance if someone else depends on your income for financial support.

If you're the primary breadwinner for a family of four, you need to buy life insurance.

If you are a single woman whose only dependent is a cat, you probably don't.

If you're a divorced mom supporting two kids, you do.

This is obvious. But the word "dependent" can encompass a variety family connections. Have you been throwing your hard-working but financially strapped sister and brother-in-law enough cash to cover their mortgage each month? Have you stashed away money for their kids' college funds? Do you have elderly parents who depend on you to supplement their meager Social Security income? Any of these people can be considered your dependents, and you may want to ensure that their financial support continues if you're no longer in the picture.

SMART MONEY

Money magazine recently noted that many insurance professionals suggest that older singles who plan to marry at some point may want to consider buying life insurance now.

Look at it this way. You are a 35-year-old man with no dependents, but you do have a fiancée. You plan to marry in a year and start a family a year or two after that.

You will likely need a life-insurance policy in the next few years, and, as a rule, term-insurance premiums jump after you hit 40. So you may want to consider locking into a level-term life-insurance policy now, while you're still young enough to get a decent rate.

Some small-business owners will even take out term life-insurance policies covering their partners. Small operations often can't survive the death of one of two or even three primary income-generators. A life-insurance policy naming your partner or partners as beneficiaries will help ensure that the business has time to regroup in the event of your death.

Insuring the Homemaker

Say you live in a household that's straight out of *Leave It to Beaver.* You are the husband, and every day you leave the house to go to work. Your wife, meanwhile, labors at home—caring for the kids, tending the garden, cleaning the house, and cooking.

You obviously need life insurance. Does she?

The answer is a resounding Maybe.

Consider this: If the family homemaker were to die tomorrow, who would take care of the kids? Who would cook? Who would clean?

Do you want to take on these responsibilities, in addition to your 9-to-5 job?

Probably not. If your wife died while the children were still young, you'd probably want to hire a child-care provider to look after the kids while you're at work; a housekeeper to keep the house tidy; and maybe even a handyman to look after your property.

If the kids have reached their teens and no longer need child care, you may feel comfortable divvying up remaining household responsibilities among family members.

If the kids are still kids, you should insure the family homemaker. A policy of $100,000 to $250,000 will usually do it.

Savvy "Homemaking" Decisions

Trish T. is a 35-year-old, full-time mom living in the suburbs of Kansas City, Missouri. She has three children: Emily, seven; Kendra, four; and Jake, two. Her husband, Paul, is mechanical engineer grossing about $93,000 per year.

When the couple sat down to look at their life-insurance needs, they seriously considered Trish's responsibilities in the family. She is perfectly healthy. But if she should suddenly be felled by an accident or unexpected illness, Paul would have to pay out a substantial amount of money to hire people who will only do for cash what Trish does out of love.

Child care was their primary concern.

"We don't have family out here," Trish said. "His parents live in Chicago. Mine live in Florida. But even if my parents or in-laws lived around the corner—well, they're getting older. I wouldn't want to burden them with [the responsibility of caring for] my children five days a week."

Besides day-to-day child care, the couple had other concerns. "Paul works really, really hard," Trish said. "I can't imagine what it would be like for him if he had to come home at night and not only look after the kids, but cook and clean as well." Couple these needs with the cost of 24-7 child care for the five or six weeks each year Paul travels on business, and the couple realized that the family's budget would tighten considerably if Trish were to die unexpectedly.

The solution? The family purchased a renewable-term $200,000, 15-year life-insurance policy for Trish. This policy falls in the typical range for homemakers—$100,000 to $250,000.

Insuring the Kids

According to Life Insurance Marketing and Research Association International, 15 percent of all life-insurance policies are bought by parents to insure their children. This is usually a waste of money. Sure, the policies can pay funeral expenses

SMART SOURCES

Be a smart shopper.
Insurance costs can
vary wildly. Get a good
deal by comparing
rates. Businesses
such as the Wholesale
Insurance Network and
the Insurance Clearing
House can give you
quotes from a variety
of different companies.

Wholesale Insurance
 Network
(800) 808-5810

Insurance Clearing
 House
(800) 472-5800

if you should sufferer the gut-wrenching loss of a child. Also, they can sometimes help ensure that a child who is presently healthy but who is later incapacitated due to accident or illness will continue with the right to buy into these plans, when he might otherwise be deemed "uninsurable." Finally, some cash-value plans out there offer the same savings component available to adults—affording your child a small nest egg.

But think about it. As noted above, you buy life insurance to continue supporting those who depend on you financially. Does anyone depend on your child for financial support?

Unless your little boy or girl is an actor supporting the rest of the family, you probably don't need to insure his or her life.

Life Insurance Types

Shopping around, you'll probably encounter two basic types of life insurance—term and cash value. Let's look at how each works.

Term Life Insurance

Term life-insurance policies cover you for a certain period of time, as long as you keep your premiums paid up. You can usually have these policies written to cover your life for the next 5-to-20 years, but policies are readily available covering you from 1 to 30 years.

The insurance company is betting that you won't die during the term of your plan. If you don't, what happens to all the premium fees you've paid? They stay with the insurance company. You will never see any money back.

If you die, cash, in the amount for which your policy is written, is paid out to those named as your beneficiaries.

There are two common types of term life insurance:

Annually Renewable Term

This is the least expensive life-insurance option, at least initially. You pay a premium each year, and your life insurance stays in effect. Premiums usually increase annually. Why? Each year you live brings you closer to death. The longer you live, the more serious a "risk" you become.

Level-Premium Term

Level-premium term costs more than annually renewable policies at first but may save you money in the long run. This is how they work: you buy a policy and agree to pay the same premium each year throughout the period of your coverage—usually 5 to 20 years. Remember: as you age, your risk of death obviously increases. When buying annually renewable term policies, you pay for that risk as you age. In level-premium term policies, you pay for that risk in equal installments over the life of your policy.

Cash-Value Policies

Cash-value policies act as insurance/investment hybrids. They are basically term-insurance policies with an investment/saving component. You pay

F.Y.I.

The Centers for Disease Control in 1998 announced that the average life expectancy for American women has hit 79.1 years; for men, 73.1 years.

the insurance company your basic premium, along with some extra money to invest for you. At your death, your heirs receive both your life-insurance benefits and the investment cash you deposited with the company. During your lifetime, you can also take loans against your investment, and even withdraw the cash outright.

Cash-value policies have a real hook: like the money you put in Individual Retirement Accounts and 401(k)s, the cash you deposit with insurance companies through cash-value policies is not taxed until you withdraw it. Therefore, these can be effective tools for high-wage earners, who have maxed out their annual yearly tax-free contributions to their IRAs.

Still, there are many, many caveats to this type of investment strategy.

1. The cash-value insurance industry enjoys nothing like a pristine reputation, these days. In the past few years, governmental bodies overseeing the insurance industry have levied fines for deceptive-sales practices against such insurance giants as MetLife, Prudential, and Allstate.

Prudential, for example, acknowledged that some of its agents convinced customers to use the cash value of older policies to buy newer, more costly coverage. Many customers lost their savings in the process.

Several states, meanwhile, charged MetLife with "churning," a process through which agents failed to tell customers that the cost of their new cash-value policies were financed with the investment components of their old policies. All their savings went to finance new, sometimes unnecessary, policies.

2. Cash-value premiums carry heavy start-up costs in their early years, eating up the investment portion of your policy, and paying you no dividends. Where does your investment portion go, at first? To the agent who sold you the policy, for his commission, and to the insurance company itself, for various start-up and "asset management" fees. Therefore, if you should choose to purchase cash-value insurance, expect to wait quite a while to see any return from your investment. Typically, at the end of your first policy year, the amount you can expect to collect should you decide to "cash out" the policy is zero. Since the premiums for cash-value policies are quite high, many money managers think it more prudent to put your cash in other moderate yield, low-risk investments.

3. Third, cash-value policies are much more expensive than term policies.

Here are some of the cash-value policies you will likely encounter when insurance shopping.

Whole Life

Whole-life policies allow you to commit to a fixed premium. Included in each premium are payments both for term-insurance coverage and a savings/investment plan. The company invests the savings portion of your premium and offers you a guaranteed rate of return. If investments have proved particularly profitable, the insurance company's governing board may declare extra dividends, and you'll enjoy a higher-than-normal rate-of-return.

F.Y.I.

The rate of return on the savings portion of whole-life premiums usually ranges from 4 to 4.5 percent.

Universal Life

These policies act very much like whole-life plans, with one key difference. Universal policies allow you to pay flexible, rather than fixed, premiums. The insurance company, of course, determines the term-insurance portion of your bill. You, however, decide how much you want to put into the savings/investment portion of your policy.

Variable Life

Like whole life and universal life, variable-life policies require you to pay a set premium for the term-insurance portion of your plan. After that, you direct the savings portion into one of the various mutual funds offered by the company. In effect, you, not the insurance company, decide where you want to invest your cash.

Survivorship Life

Survivorship life is an estate-planning insurance tool. It pays dividends not upon your death, but upon the death of a surviving spouse. Typically, this policy is bought by affluent couples. Their heirs use the benefits to pay estate taxes.

How Much Do You Need?

Many consumers find the most difficult part of buying life insurance is trying to figure out how much they actually need.

To understand how much life insurance you

should buy, you first need to determine the cash needs your family will have after your death. These include:

Immediate Needs

Your family will incur expenses immediately following your death. Your funeral is the most obvious one, but there are others. For example, your spouse will probably have to quickly pay at least some outstanding medical bills—or else suffer a blemish on her credit rating.

Income Continuation

The mortgage bill doesn't stop coming just because you've died. Neither do the electric bills, or car installment-loan payments. And you certainly don't want your death to keep your kids from going to college.

Future Expenses

Will your stay-at-home spouse decide, after your death, to enter the workforce? You may want your life insurance to pay for her continuing education. And you two had always planned to go on photo-safari in Africa. He should still have that opportunity, even if you're gone.

Will your life insurance payments have to cover all these needs? Probably not. Your spouse will likely enjoy other types of income after your death. Your life insurance need only cover the difference between your spouse's expected income after your death, and the amount of money it takes to support your family in its current style.

SMART DEFINITION

Capital gap

The difference between the amount of money it takes to support your family in its current standard of living and your surviving spouse's likely income after your death.

What Matters
• Life insurance to ensure the continued financial support of your loved ones in the event of your death. To secure this end, term policies are the best way to go.

What Doesn't
• Trying to use insurance as an investment vehicle. While cash-value policies allow you to invest money and not pay taxes until you withdraw your earnings, they are tricky to understand. If you go this route, make sure to consult a qualified financial planner.

The Formula for Determining Your Life-Insurance Needs

Use the following formula and worksheet on pages 120–21 to help determine your insurance needs.

1. Figure Out Your Current Monthly Expenses

You know what your monthly expenses are—mortgage payment, utility bills, and so forth. Take a moment now to jot down all the expenses your family currently incurs each month. Add them up. Make sure to include the following:

• Mortgage/rent payments

• Utility/phone bills

• Car payments

• Car insurance

• Food

• Credit card debts

• Health insurance

• Unreimbursed medical/dental costs

• Tuition bills (if applicable)

• Clothing

• Entertainment

- Savings

- Miscellaneous

2. Multiply These Expenses by 12 to Determine Your Annual Expenses

Take this monthly budget and multiply by 12 to determine your family's annual expenses.

3. Determine Likely Future Expenses

Life is constantly changing, and you need to take some likely changes into account when determining your insurance needs. Future expenses can include:

- Child-care costs if the person considering life insurance is the primary caregiver

- Increased health insurance premiums as the surviving spouse ages

- A move to a larger house if that is something the family has been saving for, or if your wife is pregnant at the time of your life-insurance purchase

- Children's college tuition

- Future vacations

4. Determine Monthly Revenue

Chances are, not all income will stop upon your death. Total up what your family will likely rake in after you're gone. Revenue may be expected from:

F.Y.I.

When figuring long-term expenses, don't forget the cost of inflation. As a general rule, you want to add 4 percent per year to your current expenses to account for it.

F.Y.I.

You're learning to account for future expenses to help determine your life-insurance needs. But you may find yourself in a situation when, in only a few years, your expenses will decrease. For example, if your current mortgage will be paid off in two years, or if your last child has only a year of college to go, remember to subtract these expenses while determining your family's future budget.

SMART SOURCES

Your surviving spouse and minor children are probably entitled to Social Security benefits upon your death. To determine how much they are eligible for, call Social Security and ask for a Record of Earnings and Estimate of Benefits statement.

Social Security
(800) 772-1213

- The salary of the surviving spouse

- Social Security benefits paid to your surviving spouse and minor children

- Dividends from current investments

- Pension payments paid to your spouse after your death

5. Multiply Total Monthly Revenue by 12 to Determine Your Annual Revenue

6. Determine Your Capital Gap

Determine the amount of money your family needs each year, taking into account likely increasing expenses (for example, college tuition) or decreasing expenses (say, paying off the mortgage) and inflation. Deduct from this total the yearly revenues gleaned from expected sources of support. The difference is your *capital gap*.

7. Determine the Number of Years You'll Want to Provide Support for Your Family

Once you have determined your yearly capital gap, talk with your spouse about how long you want your life insurance to support your family. Perhaps you'll only want it for 10 years—by then your kids will be out of school and your wife can survive very nicely on her salary as a corporate attorney. Perhaps your spouse is untrained, unskilled, and has no desire to ever enter the workforce, and you want to support him for a much longer period.

8. Multiply Your Capital Gap by the Number of Years You Want to Support Your Family

Multiply the capital gap by the number of years you wish to support your family. That's roughly the minimum amount of life insurance you want to buy—your *base policy amount.*

9. Add Your Total Future Expenses (from Step 3) to Your Base Policy Amount

This number represents your ideal total-insurance-coverage amount. Beware: the difference between minimum (base policy amount) and ideal (total coverage) will cost you.

If you're afraid that your life insurance benefits coupled with your other assets will subject your estate to hefty taxes, reread chapter 4. You'll learn how an irrevocable life-insurance trust bypasses estate taxes.

The formula for determining your life-insurance needs should be considered a general guideline only. Talk to a competent financial planner about your specific situation.

Use the sample worksheet on the following pages as a model to help you set down your own unique circumstances to paper. Then, plug in the formula to get a ballpark figure of life insurance needs for you and your family before checking with a financial planner.

Determine How Much Life Insurance You Need

Step 1: Determine Monthly Expenses.
Each month, we spend . . .

Expenditure	*Amount*
Mortgage/rent	_____
Utility/phone bills	_____
Car payments	_____
Car insurance	_____
Food	_____
Credit card payments	_____
Health insurance	_____
Unreimbursed medical/dental costs	_____
Tuition bills	_____
Clothing	_____
Entertainment	_____
Savings	_____
Miscellaneous	_____
Total Monthly Expenses:	_____

Step 2: Multiply Total Monthly Expenses by 12 to Determine Total Annual Expenses.

Total Annual Expenses: _____

Step 3: Determine Likely Future Expenses.
My life insurance policy should also cover:

Expense	*Amount*
Childcare	_____
Increased health insurance premiums	_____
A move to a larger house	_____
College tuition, child A	_____
College tuition, child B	_____
College tuition, child C	_____
Vacations	_____
Other expenses	_____
Total Future Expenses:	_____

Step 4: Determine Monthly Revenue.
After my death, my family will receive the following cash each month:

Revenue	Amount
Salary of surviving spouse	_____
Social Security benefits to	_____
surviving spouse	_____
Social Security benefits for child A	_____
Social Security benefits for child B	_____
Social Security benefits for child C	_____
Dividends from current investments	_____
Pension payments	_____
Total Monthly Revenue:	_____

Step 5: Multiply Total Monthly Revenue by 12 to Determine Total Annual Revenue.

Total Annual Revenue: _____

Step 6: Subtract Total Annual Revenue from Total Annual Expenditures. (This is your Yearly Capital Cap.)

Yearly Capital Gap: _____

Step 7: Determine the Number of Years You'll Want to Support Your Family.

Total Years of Support: _____

Step 8: Multiply Your Yearly Capital Gap by the Number of Years for Which You'll Want to Support Your Family. (This is your Base Policy Amount.)

Base Policy Amount: _____

Step 9: Add Your Total Future Expenses (from Step 3) to Your Base Policy Amount. This figure represents your Total Insurance Needs, and you should attempt to buy a policy to cover this amount.

Total Insurance Needs: _____

Private Nursing Home Insurance

Nothing can eat up your potential estate faster than your need for long-term care. Medicaid, a government entitlement program, will pay for nursing home care only if government deems you "impoverished." You and your spouse may have to spend the majority of the cash you've saved over the years toward nursing home care before the government decides you are "poor enough" and allows you to claim Medicaid insurance. That's why privately sold nursing home insurance has grown so popular in recent years.

A Nursing Home Insurance Caveat

These premiums are not cheap. They run, on average, $2,000 a year, and premiums of up to $4,000 or even $6,000 a year are not uncommon. Cost varies in accordance with a number of factors:

• **Your age and health.** As with many types of insurance, the older and sicker you are, the higher your premium.

• **Elimination period.** The "elimination period" is similar to a deductible in other insurance policies. Your car insurance may carry a $500 deductible, meaning you pay for repairs to the first $500 worth of damage done to your automobile. Only once repair costs exceed that cap does your insurance kick in. The elimination period in nursing home policies requires you to pay for the beginning of your stay on your own, before the benefits of your policy go into effect. Common options are 30, 60, and 90 days of self-pay. They longer your elimination period, the lower your premiums.

• **Daily benefit.** This is the amount of money your policy will pay for each day of your stay in a nursing home. To determine how high a daily benefit you will need, contact a number of nursing homes in your area to see what they charge. Again, the higher your daily benefit, the higher your premium.

• **Benefit period.** You can write nursing home insurance policies to cover your expected length of stay in a nursing home. Benefit periods run from one year to the remainder of life. The longer your benefit period, the higher your premium.

Do You Need It?

If you're an older American with no savings, and therefore no cash to contribute to your nursing home stay, Medicaid will take care of it. You don't need private insurance.

Experts say you should consider buying nursing home insurance if you're a retired American enjoying an annual income of at least $30,000 per year, with assets, excluding your home, of at least $100,000.

F.Y.I.

The average nursing home stay runs three years.

THE BOTTOM LINE

If anyone depends on you for financial support, you need to purchase life insurance. You want your life-insurance policy to ensure the continued financial support of your loved ones in the event of your death. You'll find a variety of term- and cash-value policies available. Cash-value policies allow you to invest money along with your premiums and not pay taxes until you withdraw your earnings. But you don't need to use insurance plans as investment tools. The difference between the amount of money your family needs to live in its current style and the amount the family will likely take in in the event of your death, is called a capital gap. Your life insurance should cover this difference.

A Final Word . . .

Life insurance is only one way to take care of your family. As unpleasant as it is to contemplate, you must begin to think about who will take care of your minor children in the event of your death. This issue is discussed thoroughly in the next chapter, as is how to best pass on your family business and how to set up trusts for children incapable of handling money.

CHAPTER 7

·····················

All in the Family

Your will. Throughout this book, you've come to think of it as a legal document delineating which of your heirs get what. And you're right.

But now, for a minute, think of your will as your intention. What do you care about most? For most people, it's families and careers. In this chapter, we'll examine ways to provide for your minor children and to ensure the continued success of your business in the event of your death. Plan for them in accordance with your will.

Appointing a Guardian

In chapter 2, you learned some equitable ways to pass on family valuables. But your concern about who gets your great-grandfather's pocket watch or Aunt Maybel's pottery collection probably pales in comparison to your chief worry: Who gets your minor children?

Married couples worry about who will get their children in the event of their simultaneous death—car crashes, plane crashes, other acts of God. Single parents with absent spouses worry about their own deaths. Both types of parents fret about their children's continued emotional and financial support.

Chances are you'll not only live to see your kids grow up but also get to spend some quality time with your grandchildren. But just in case you should get hit by lightning while the kids are still small—you need to appoint a personal guardian to watch out for them in a daily basis. You will also need to appoint someone to handle the monetary bequests you leave to the child.

In a best-case scenario, those two responsibilities fall to the same person.

You'll learn about handling your child's money later in the chapter. For now, let's talk about how you go about naming a personal guardian.

Appointing a Personal Guardian: What the Heart Says

The act of choosing a personal guardian for your child is apt to prove very emotional. You don't want to die. And you certainly don't want to die before your kids reach adulthood. But if something unexpected should happen, you want to make sure that your children will continue to enjoy a loving and stable home life.

This is how you put the process in motion.

First, sit down with a piece of paper and think of what you want for your children. Their growing up in a traditional, two-parent home may be important to you. Stability and continuity definitely are. You might want the kids raised by a member of your immediate family, because you appreciate and respect the clan's history and heritage. You may want your children to grow up with the same sense of roots. Of course, you want your kids to have lots of love. You want them raised with the values to which you adhere. And their education is likely very, very important to you. Jot down your "wish list" for your children. Then list all the people who

F.Y.I.

Your "children" are your offspring. You can be a 100-year-old mother with an 80-year-old child. Your "minor children" are offspring under the age of 18.

If two parents are divorced, and the parent with primary custody of the children dies, full custody almost always transfers to the surviving parent.

SMART DEFINITION

Personal guardian

Someone legally responsible for raising your child. A person legally responsible for managing your child's assets is called a "custodian," "trustee," or "property guardian."

F.Y.I.

U.S. News & World Report recently estimated that including college tuition, the cost of raising a child in a middle-income family has hit $1.45 million.

you think could likely fulfill these wishes. Parents, siblings, and beloved friends will probably all appear on the list.

Then whittle that list, taking the following criteria into account:

• **Emotional stability.** You want someone with the temperament to raise your wonderful, but somewhat rambunctious, two-year-old twins.

• **Religious affiliation.** Religious heritage is very, very important to many people. If you are a devout Orthodox Jew, you may not want your child raised by a Catholic best friend.

• **Financial stability.** Sure, you may have enough money to financially care for your kids after your death. But suppose your estate is very modest? You do not want your kids to become an undue financial burden on their new guardians. You do not want your children raised in an atmosphere of resentment.

• **Moral Code.** Determine which of your child's potential guardians embrace a moral code you respect.

• **Age.** You may have been raised by the most wonderful parents in the world. Thankfully, they're both still around to enjoy your children. But they're in their mid-60s, now. Do they really have the strength to look after your pre-teens? And what happens when they begin to develop their own health problems? Finally, parenting is hard work—grand-parenting is pure joy. You may think that your parents have earned the right to simple grandparenthood.

The Trouble with "Heartfelt"

Sarah looked at her friend Lois and asked, "If anything happened to Pete and I, would you take care of Elizabeth?"

Sarah's friend couldn't believe her ears—she was so flattered. "Of course I will," she said. "Of course."

Sarah was 25; Lois, 24. They'd known each other for more than a decade—since Lois's first day of high school. Their relationship had only deepened as they aged. They were closer to each other than to their own siblings. In some ways, they were closer to each other than to their lovers and spouses.

Sarah had married young, to an oil-company junior executive. Before her daughter, Elizabeth, now an infant, was born, she'd worked as a personal assistant to a car dealership president. Peter and Sarah, between them, grossed around $60,000 a year, but they hadn't saved much.

Lois was a single woman, a reporter at a regional daily newspaper in Pennsylvania. After taxes, she brought home about $20,000 a year. She lived with a roommate in a ramshackle country house, replete with a golden retriever and a couple of cats. The stove hadn't worked for three months. Nobody really noticed.

"I really loved Sarah," Lois said recently. "And I adored Elizabeth. I thought that I could take good care of her, if, God forbid, something should happen to both her parents. But the next day, when I told my mom that I was going to be named Elizabeth's personal guardian, she said I was crazy."

After that phone call, Lois really looked at her life . She was having lots of fun. If called upon, she had much to offer a child emotionally, but it would mean a complete rearrangement of her life—a rearrangement she might come to resent. Worse, she was only making $20,000 a year. Though Sarah and Peter lived comfortably, they had not yet set away too much in savings, so she couldn't count on their bequest to help her out financially. In addition, they had yet to purchase life insurance.

Lois was, in short, emotionally and financially incapable of caring for Elizabeth at this stage in her life.

She was dumb to have initially accepted this responsibility. Frankly, Sarah was dumb to have asked. Sarah eventually named her older brother, a well-established photographer, as Elizabeth's personal guardian.

• **Willingness.** Choose someone who actually wants to raise kids—and who wants to raise your kids, if called upon.

Whittle down your list by deciding which of your relatives and friends meet the criteria listed above. Talk to the people you're still considering. Figure out who is willing to do the job—and make sure prospective guardians understand all the ramifications of your decision. Don't let anyone off with a laugh—believing that, since you're only 35, they'll never be called into duty.

Appointing a Personal Guardian: The Legalities

You must name your child's personal guardian in your will in order for that person to end up actually raising your child in the event of your death.

You should:

• Make sure the guardian understands the ramifications of this decision.

• Name an alternate guardian just in case the life circumstances of your first choice change dramatically around the time of your death.

• Name only one person even if the child will likely be raised by a married couple. This means that you should appoint only "Jane Doe" not "Mr. and Mrs. John Doe" as your child's personal guardian. Do this in case a married couple divorces. You don't want your child to become the subject of a nasty custody fight.

• If necessary, you can name a different guardian for each child. Of course, you will probably want your children raised together, but, especially if you have several kids, you may have no choice but to name several guardians.

• Name a separate property manager to handle your child's assets—but only if absolutely necessary. (You'll learn more about this later in the chapter.)

Your express wishes do not make the transfer of custody a sure thing. After your death, a judge will determine whether the person you have named is fit to serve as a parent. This is usually a pro-forma decision, but there is always the outside chance that the judge may find your personal guardian unfit to serve as a parent. If the personal guardian you named is found to be unfit—if, say, she has a serious criminal history, instances of child abuse or sexual abuse in her background, or an active alcohol or drug addiction—the judge may appoint another guardian. Of course, though, nobody loves your kids the way you do—and you're unlikely to leave them in the care of an active alcoholic who regularly mistreats her own children.

Occasionally, other family members may challenge your choice of personal guardian. Unless they have a truly substantive reason for doing so, your choice of personal guardian will usually prevail.

Here's an example:

You and your husband die in a car crash, and your will has named your younger sister, Jane, as the kids' personal guardian. If your parents challenge your choice solely because they are bigots, angry with Jane because she has chosen to marry outside her race, and they don't want their grandchildren raised in an "mixed" relationship—they probably don't stand a chance of getting your kids.

But turn this scenario around. Suppose your parents love Jane and her husband with all their hearts, but they know something that you don't. Namely, that Jane has, over the last few years, developed a nasty, untreated cocaine problem. In fact, she has turned to petty larceny to support this habit. The judge, deciding in the best interest of the children, may well decide that Jane is not the best person to care for your kids at this time of her life.

After all this, the actual clause in your will in which you appoint your child's personal guardian and property guardian (discussed below) is very simple. This is what former Beatle John Lennon wrote: "I nominate, constitute and appoint my wife Yoko Ono as the Guardian of the person and property of any children of the marriage who may survive me. In the event that she predeceases me, or for any reason she chooses not to act in that capacity, I nominate, constitute and appoint Sam Green to act in her place and stead."

Property Guardians

After choosing a personal guardian, you need to appoint a property guardian to manage the assets you've left, for your child, in your estate.

As noted above, the person legally responsible for managing your child's assets is called a property guardian. Legally, he is charged with "collecting, holding, investing, and reinvesting" the estates for the benefit of the minor, and he is entitled to reasonable compensation for his work.

In a best-case scenario, you should choose the

A Cautionary Tale

It's generally a bad idea to appoint one person to care for your child's person and another for his or her assets. Consider the latest chapter in the saga of the legendary Onassis family:

When Christina Onassis, sole adult heir to the Onassis shipping fortune, died of heart failure in 1988, she left behind her daughter, Athina, then a toddler, and an estate valued at more than $5 billion.

Upon Christina's death, her ex-husband and Athina's dad, Thierry Roussel, took custody of the child.

But Athina's inheritance—Christina's $5 billion estate—fell under the control of four of Christina's trusted financial advisers and family confidants, who were charged with managing Athina's inheritance until she turned 21.

Christina's decision to divide the responsibility for Athina's care in such a way has made for a rough-and-tumble decade, with Roussel and the four men who actually control Athina's inheritance constantly at loggerheads. The trustees, who are fiercely loyal to the memory and wishes of the late Onassis family, argue that the $13 million Roussel receives each year to raise his daughter should pretty much suffice for her needs. Roussel, on the other hand, regularly argues—and sometimes sues—for a larger allowance, and a greater say in the management of his daughter's inheritance.

And Athina herself? So far, she seems just to be trying to lead the normal life her own mother never had—and probably has to cover her ears while the grown-ups argue loudly over her money.

The lesson for the rest of us regular folks is that if you can appoint the same person to serve as both personal and property guardian for your child, by all means do so.

same person to be both your child's personal guardian and property guardian. If you do not think that the person most emotionally suited to raising your child can possibly handle your child's assets—feel free to appoint a separate property garden. Beware, though: conflicts of interest can arise between the two.

Consider this scenario:

You child's school district seems to be going down hill. His personal guardian thinks it best to shell out $5,000 per year to send him to a private academy. The property guardian, a great believer in the public school system, thinks this is a foolish expenditure.

Clearly, the child's personal guardian—the person who lives with him, cares for him each day, and checks his homework—has a firmer grasp of the child's needs than does the property guardian. The personal guardian's decision should probably prevail in this case. But he needs cash to implement this decision, and the property guardian won't allot it.

Trusts to Provide for Your Child

You can't leave your entire $200,000 estate to your 14-year-old outright, even if you *want* it spent on video games and Nikes. Most states place stringent limits on how much money a minor can hold on his own.

In most cases, you have three vehicles that you can use to hold money for the child. They are the Uniform Transfer to Minors Act (UTMA), aChild's

Trust, and a Family Pot Trust. Special trusts for children with disabilities, or adult children incapable of handling money, are discussed in the next section. UTMAs, child's trusts and family pot trusts can be set up now, to take effect only in the event of your death.

Unlike other trusts, trusts for children are not meant to skirt taxes or force an irresponsible adult to make prudent use of your money. Rather, they are meant solely to ensure the continued financial support of your child, until such time as you (or the state) deem him responsible enough to handle the cash on his own. Also, trusts for children allow the trustee to regularly use the principal—as long as such use is necessary for the support of the minor child.

F.Y.I.

State limitation in how much money a minor can control outright range from $1,000 to $5,000.

Uniform Transfer to Minors Act (UTMA)

Forty-seven states and the District of Columbia allow parents to pass assets on to their children via the Uniform Transfer to Minors Act. UTMAs can not be used in Michigan, South Carolina, or Vermont.

They work this way:

You write up your will, stating what property you are leaving to your child. You name a property guardian (often the same person as the personal guardian). The property guardian "collects, holds, invests, and reinvests" the money until the child turns 18 or 21, depending on the state in which he resides. At that age, the estate becomes the child's outright.

The problem with a UTMA is that it demands

your child receive estate properties outright when he reaches 18 or 21. Lots of kids are simply not mature enough, at these ages, to handle substantial funds.

Child's Trust

A child's trust allows you to state, in your will, exactly what property you're leaving to which child. A property guardian holds this cash in trust for the support of each of your offspring.

If you have a $200,000 estate and two children, the most common scenario would entail your leaving $100,000 in trust for each child.

Unlike an UTMA, a child's trust allows you—not the state—to determine when your offspring can take full control of their assets. You may think that a young adult of 18, 21, or even 25 is too young to make decisions involving a substantive amount of cash. You may decide not to turn the trust assets over to the child's control until he reaches the age of 30, or even 35—whatever age you deem appropriate.

There can be problem's with a child's trust, though. As noted above, you decide how much property you're leaving each of your offspring. But not all children lead equal lives. A child, through no fault of his own, may need more cash than one of his siblings. His guardian, however, cannot access the funds you've left behind for one child for the support of another. That's why some families prefer family pot trusts.

Family Pot Trust

A family pot trust differs from a child's trust in that it allows you to leave your entire estate to benefit all your children—you do not need to determine which of your offspring gets which property.

This type of trust can prove a benefit if, for some reason, the financial needs of one child outstrip the needs of his siblings.

Take the following as an example:

You have three children—Britt, Matthew, and Anna. You and your husband die unexpectedly, leaving behind a $300,000 estate.

Britt, tragically, is severely injured in a car crash. His health insurance pays for his medical care, but not for his occupational training. A family pot trust allows Britt's guardian to dip into the entire estate—not just Britt's supposed pro-rata $100,000 share—to pay for that therapy.

As with a child's trust, a family pot trust allows you to determine at what age assets are passed, outright, to your offspring. This is usually based on the age of the youngest child. For example, in the case above, the trust may have been written to indicate that assets pass outright to Britt, Matthew, and Anna when Anna, the youngest, reaches age 21.

This can be a problem, though, if there's a significant age gap among your children. Say you have a 16-year-old, a 5-year-old, and a 3-year-old. Should the eldest really have to wait to take control of your assets until the baby turns 21? Probably not. He'd be 34 by then. One way to avoid this is to establish a separate child's trust for each of your kids, or to establish a child's trust for the eldest, with a family pot trust covering the younger two. Talk to a qualified estate lawyer.

F.Y.I.

Conflicts of interest can arise if a healthy sibling is appointed property guardian for a disabled child. Typically, provisions in property control trusts call for trust assets to be passed on to a deceased parent's healthy kids after the death of the disabled child. Therefore, a sibling acting as property guardian may sometimes want to pay out as little as possible for his disabled brother or sister, hoping to save as much of the trust funds as possible for his own eventual enjoyment.

Families Members with Special Concerns

You have a son with Down's syndrome, or muscular dystrophy, or another catastrophic illness that makes it either highly unlikely or impossible for him to ever be able to handle money.

The Property Control Trust or the Irrevocable Protection Trust is a specific trust that can ensure that your special-needs child receives the cash he needs to live comfortably, without the responsibility of money management.

Property Control Trust or the Irrevocable Protection Trust

As with the trusts discussed above, you appoint a property guardian to handle your disabled child's share of your estate. These trusts normally run for the life of the child. (You can't expect that a child suffering with Down's syndrome to miraculously be cured at the age of 21, or 25, or 35, or sadly, ever.) The property guardian may be a healthy sibling, or, to avoid conflicts of interest, you may want to go with a bank trust department. If necessary, you may also appoint a personal guardian to look after the child's needs. A final beneficiary can be named to receive the remainder of the trust funds after the child's death.

The property guardian pays, from the trust, your child's day-to-day expenses, and makes determinations about extraordinary costs. For example, suppose you have a child living in a group home.

The home has planned to take some residents on a hiking trip to Yosemite National Park. Can your child afford to go? The property guardian will make that determination.

If you have a child with a potentially "curable" illness or disability, you may want to include codicils in your trust allowing for the child to take control of estate assets in the event of his cure. Say, for an example, your child is a seemingly hopeless schizophrenic. Then a new drug comes along that, when taken properly, allows him to act in a mature and responsible manner. You may want to add a codicil to your trust stating that, once the child has acted responsibly for a period of three years, (as determined by the property guardian) the trust assets revert to your child outright.

If you have an adult child with no clear disability, but who just seems incapable of handling money in a mature manner, you might consider setting up a trust for his or her welfare. Trusts are discussed in more detail in chapter 4.

F.Y.I.

If you are putting your assets into an Irrevocable Protection Trust for your child because you simply don't trust his or her spouse, you may consider adding certain codicils that will allow your child to take complete control of his inheritance in the event of divorce, or the death of his spouse.

Trusts versus Social Security

You may have a child whose disability enables him to receive supplemental security income—a form of Social Security meant to provide shelter, clothing, and food to the disabled. You fear that leaving the child an inheritance will mean he has too much income to to qualify for these benefits. On the other hand, you certainly don't want your child living only the bare-bones existence that SSI provides.

A certain trust, called the Special Needs Trust, can guide you out of this conundrum.

It works like this: You set up a trust to cover expenses other than the basic food, clothing, and shelter needs that SSI covers. You appoint a third party trustee to administer it.

Since the trust can not be used for food, clothing, and shelter, your child will not lose his SSI benefits. Trust funds, however, can be doled out by the trustee to ensure the extras that make life enjoyable—vacations, outings, and other things that you'd probably want the child to have. Talk to a lawyer about setting up this type of trust.

Your Grandchildren versus Your In-Laws

Every state allows you to leave your assets to your married child only—meaning you don't have to leave any money to your child's spouse.

That's fine, in theory. But problems arise in many healthy marriages when the beneficiary of your will shares his inheritance with his spouse. Your daughter-in-law's name goes on the deed to any real property you leave. Any cash assets go into the marital pot.

You may be very fond of your daughter-in-law, but you adore your grandkids. You want your assets to pass to them in the event of your son's death.

If your son has chosen to control your assets jointly with his wife, she will probably end up with all the fruits of your hard labor in the event of your son's death. If your son dies young, your daughter-in-law may marry again, and your assets ultimately end up being split among your grandchildren and your daughter-in-law's three step-children from her second marriage.

If this scenario worries you, consider the Living Trust or the Irrevocable Protection Trust to avoid it.

The Living Trust

Consider leaving your cash in a living trust for your child, naming her as both the beneficiary and the trustee, with her children as ultimate beneficiary. This setup gives her the right to both manage trusts assets, and spend them for any purpose. It does not guarantee that she won't use trust benefits for the support of a husband who refuses to get a job—but it does guarantee that any assets left over at the end of her life will pass to your grandchildren.

The Irrevocable Protection Trust

If you believe that you son's spouse is too manipulative or irresponsible to come near your inheritance, you may consider setting up an Irrevocable Protection Trust. Name your child as the beneficiary, and appoint a third party (for example, a bank trust department) as trustee. The trustee will dole out funds for your day-to-day support, with additional funds allowed for occasional "enjoyment of life" situations, such as vacations. Your child will have no control over the disbursement of this cash, and, at his or her death, remaining assets will pass to any ultimate beneficiaries you have named—in this case, your grandchildren.

SMART SOURCES

The National Family Business Council is a private consulting and research group based in Lake Forest, Illinois. Its employees consult with the owners of family-owned businesses nationwide.

1640 West Kennedy Blvd.
Lake Forest, IL 60045
(847) 295-1040

SMART MONEY

Lawyers Gerald M. Condon and Jeffrey L. Condon note in their book *Beyond the Grave: The Right Way and the Wrong Way of Leaving Money to Your Children (and Others)* that two out of three family businesses do not survive the death of the founder.

Passing On the Family Business

Of all the assets you have to disperse, the equitable division of your family business may prove the most problematic. Unlike the division of other assets, it is often not a good idea to equally divide a business among your children.

Why?

You'll more than likely want the business to continue to succeed, and not all of your children likely have the ability, or the desire, to run the family concern.

Suppose you're Joe Smith, owner of Joe's Carpet Cleaning, Inc. You have three children—two sons and a daughter. Your daughter has entered the family concern, applying all the knowledge she gleaned while working toward her MBA to double, then triple, Joe's business. Your sons, meanwhile, have pursued careers in carpentry and teaching. Neither knows anything about Joe's Carpet Cleaning's machinations.

Leaving your business equally to your three equally loved children is, in this case, a bad idea. First, your sons have no idea how Joe's works. Your daughter does. Her say in the management of this business should exceed your boys'. Second, your daughter is currently working very hard to increase Joe's overall sales. Why should she work to increase the profits of a business, when she will eventually be forced to share the fruits of her labors with her brothers?

This may seem obvious to you, but, as noted throughout this book, without frank discussions of why you are leaving certain assets to certain offspring, your heirs will likely look at their piece of your legacy as a barometer of your love—especially with as valuable an asset as the family business. To continue the scenario presented above, if Joe's sons learn for the first time at the reading of their father's will that their sister has been left the family business, they will likely not consider her MBA, or her on-the-job training. They well think, "See! Well, Dad always loved her best."

To help ensure that your business continues to operate after your death, and to avoid hurt feelings among your relatives, you should put in place a succession plan.

The Succession Plan

You should plan for the future of your business as carefully as you plan the rest of your estate.

To determine how your business will pass into the hands of, and provide for, your next generation, you should:

• Establish a committee to oversee the succession of your business. It should consist of family members and professionals such as lawyers and family-business consultants. The presence of these impartial outside experts can be invaluable in avoiding hurt feelings.

• Call a family meeting, or series of meetings, to discuss each child's future role, if any, in the business. Be realistic. If your son, a carpenter, says he hopes to take the helm of your computer-consulting firm, insist that he train in the computer and business-management fields.

F.Y.I.

According to the Family Business Center in Chicago, nearly half the nation's gross domestic product is produced by family businesses. And anywhere from 10 to 20 million such enterprises now operate in the United States.

SMART DEFINITION

Succession agreement

A formal, binding document that outlines to whom your business will pass, and which heir will enjoy what percentage of ownership in your business. Consider having one drawn up by a lawyer.

• Determine transfer of ownership if more than one child plans to play a role in the business. He or she may change career plans later on. In general, you want to give children who choose to remain in the business the right to "buy out" the shares held by the exiting family member.

• Determine whether children who are not involved in the business should be able to claim a share of its profits.

• Discuss and determine compensation in your estate for children who choose not to take part in the family business. (In an ideal world, you would leave them assets equal to the value of your business. See below for more information.)

A Case of "Father Knows Best"

Harry J. started a family business years ago, and lived long enough to see his three sons rise in the company. He actually lived long enough to see them have knock-down, drag-out fights every week. And he knew that they wouldn't be able to run the business together when he wasn't around to pound his fist on the desk and put an end to the nonsense.

So Harry employed the trust department of a bank to oversee the business for seven years after his death. In short, the bank played Daddy. When Harry died, his sons continued to duke it out over every decision. But they fought in a bank boardroom. Year after year they wrangled, but, gradually, they calmed down. They started to present a unified front to the bank trustees. By year five, they'd learned to get along. By year seven, they ran the business as a team. Their father's foresight prevented the loss of the business and ensured the continued success of it, and therefore, the continued financial support of his family.

In general, to ensure the continued growth of the family business after your death, you may want to consider one of the following moves as your succession plan:

- **Leave your business only to the child who has labored for it.** Leave your daughter Joe's Carpet Cleaning Inc. and leave each of your sons other assets worth about the same as the family business.

- **Sell the business to the child working in it.** You can avoid estate hassles by allowing your business child to buy your business now, and leaving all remaining assets to your children equally. This can prove especially important if you have no other assets equal to your business—and your decision to leave that concern to one child will seem like an act of favoritism. It can help your assets avoid estate taxes by transferring a significant asset into the hands of a member of the younger generation—who will likely outlive you by decades. (For a further discussion of tax issues, see chapter 3.) Finally, a lawyer can write the terms of sale in such a way to continue to afford you an income from the business, ensuring that you enjoy a financially comfortable old age.

- **Leaving the business in trust for the children, appointing an impartial outsider (such as a bank trust department) to oversee operations.** If you are leaving the business to more than one child, and they have already learned to work as a team, terrific. If you suspect that your children will be unable to work for the common good after your death, you may consider leaving it in a trust for a set number of years, until your children learn to work together in the business's best interests.

What Matters

• Trust your head, heart, and gut when providing for the continued financial support of your minor children.

• Selecting a guardian for your child is your decision, regardless of what others think. What matters is appointing a person who will give your child the best home life possible.

• Planning for the future of your business as a continued source of income for your heirs.

What Doesn't

• Hurt feelings among your relatives when deciding who should raise your minor child.

• When planning for the future of your business, giving an unmotivated or uninterested child a secure job for life.

On the Home Front

Next to the division of your business, questions surrounding the division of the family home are most likely to cause consternation among your beneficiaries.

Many Americans count the family home as their most valuable asset. However, in the age of the mobile society, the home place does not have the sentimental value that it once did. Plenty of kids will be perfectly happy to sell the place and split the proceeds equally after Mom and Dad pass on.

Problems can arise, though, if the house has sentimental meaning for one child—leading him to want to keep the place for himself—when the other children want to take their share of the property in cash. The child who wants the place can, in this scenario, buy out his siblings—assuming, of course, he has the cash.

As noted earlier in this book, it's usually best to divide your assets evenly among your children. Therefore, if you have one child who wants the house, you can usually leave it to him solely, without acrimony, only if you have assets of equal value to distribute among your remaining children.

All these scenarios entail a traditional nuclear family. Special issues often arise when the home in which you raised your children you now share with a husband other than the kids' dad.

Your children believe they have the right to inherit the house when you die—even if it means evicting the stepparent from his home. Your husband, meanwhile, has expressed his desire to remain in the marital home, even after your death.

What to do?

You can place the house in trust, naming your

spouse as the life beneficiary. This gives him the right to live in the home until his own death. Name your children as final beneficiaries—they will take control of the property after your spouse's death and decide the fate of the house as they wish.

By now, you should have a handle on the fundamentals of estate planning. But don't forget the last chapter—on writing a living will, an ethical will, and prepaying for and planning your funeral. These preparations will help make your last days on the planet as stress free as possible.

THE BOTTOM LINE

When you're considering your family's future welfare, you must take into consideration the emotional and financial support of your minor children; the continuation of financial support for adult offspring who are incapable of managing money themselves; how to keep your assets in your bloodline, if you are uncomfortable with the prospect of your in-laws receiving them; and how to equitably pass on a family business.

When providing for the continued financial support of your minor children, or for the succession of your business, you need to trust your head, your heart, and your gut. These are your decisions. Hurt feelings are unimportant, but planning for the future of your business and a continued source of income for your heirs is important.

Planning for a Change

So far, reading this book, you've learned how to care for your loved ones after your death. Now it's time to think, for a moment, about caring for yourself as your life draws to its close.

Death and Dying: Have It Your Way

If you're like many people, you fear death less than you fear the way in which you will die. You can accept your inevitable end, but you can't stand the idea of lying around in an irreversible coma for years, a constant source of stress and sadness to your family and friends, alive only because a ventilator keeps breathing for you.

You can ensure that your desires about what medical care you wish to receive or avoid are followed by writing a living will, and providing someone you trust with a durable power of attorney to execute it.

Advance Directives

According to the U.S. Department of Health and Human Services, you can decide in advance what medical treatment you want to receive if you become physically or mentally unable to communicate your wishes. In addition, you enjoy certain rights as an adult patient in a hospital, skilled nursing facility, or other health-care setting.

Your Rights as a Patient

• To keep your personal and medical records private;

• To know what kind of medical treatment you will receive; and

• To tell people ahead of time what type of treatment you want, or don't want in case you lose the ability to speak for yourself.

You can exercise these rights by preparing an Advance Directive, which is a written document that tells people how to make your medical decisions when you can't make them for yourself. An Advance Directive can also designate someone else to make medical decisions for you. Two common Advance Directives are a living will and a durable power of attorney for health care.

Living Will

A living will is a legal document through which you state what medical treatment you want offered and what you want withheld. It is called a living will because it takes effect while you are still living. Generally, in the event you should suffer an irreversible coma or face "imminent death" from a terminal illness, the will allows you to speak now, in preparation for a time when you will be unable to speak for yourself.

Your living will covers procedures that will prolong your life but not cure you. Typically, the document requests some form of the following:

SMART DEFINITION

Living will

Depending on the state in which you reside, a living will may also be called a Durable Power of Attorney for Heath Care; Medical Directive; Directive to Physicians; Declaration Regarding Health Care; or Designation of Health Care Surrogate.

Imminent death

Many states consider death to be "imminent" when physicians have determined that you have less than 30 days to live.

Sample Living Will

DIRECTIVE MADE this _____ day of _____, 2000, to my physicians, my attorneys, my clergyman, my family or others responsible for my health, welfare or affairs.

BE IT KNOWN that I, _____ of the State of _____, being an adult of sound mind, willfully and voluntarily make this statement as a directive to be followed if I am in a terminal condition and become unable to participate in decisions regarding my health care. I understand that my health-care providers are legally bound to act consistently with my wishes, within the limits of responsible medical practice and other applicable law. I also understand that I have the right to make medical and health care decisions for myself as long as I am able to do so and to revoke this declaration at any time.

_____   _____
Signature   Address

Signed in the presence of:

_____   _____
Witness   Address

_____   _____
Witness   Address

- All life-prolonging measures be rendered;

- All life-prolonging measures be withheld; or

- Some mixture thereof;

- That you be provided with "comfort care," including pain medication.

Many living will forms list the most common life-prolonging procedures, allowing you to pick and choose which you want administered and which you want withheld. For example, it is not uncommon for people to say that they don't want a ventilator to prolong their lives, but, if necessary, will allow a surgery to implant a feeding tube if such a measure is necessary for them to continue to receive sustenance.

These forms allow you to make decisions well ahead of your final illness—and that's great. But, perhaps as important, they relieve your family of the burden of making painful decisions about the continuation of your life.

Durable Power of Attorney for Health Care

A durable power of attorney for health care allows you to appoint someone to ensure that health-care providers give you the medical care you want and withhold the care you don't. This document takes the form of a signed, dated, and witnessed paper authorizing another person to make your medical decisions.

Your attorney—in this cases, the word means anyone authorized by you to work on your behalf in health-care matters—following your wishes, decides which treatment should be imparted, which treatment should be withheld, whether you should receive pain medication, and whether you should undergo surgery that may prolong your life but not cure you. Working in this capacity, your attorney has the ability to hire and fire your health-care workers, look at your medical files, and act on your

F.Y.I.

In a 1990 right-to-die case, the U.S. Supreme Court decided that every American has the right to control his own medical care, and in cases where a patient is incapacitated, health-care providers must follow "clear and convincing evidence of those wishes" when determining what treatment to allow and what to withhold.

F.Y.I.

Federal law requires hospitals, skilled nursing facilities, hospices, home health agencies, and managed care plans to give their patients who are covered by Medicare or Medicaid information about Advanced Directives.

Sample Durable Power of Attorney for Health Care

I understand that my wishes expressed in the following cases may not cover all possible aspects of my care if I become incompetent. I also may be undecided about whether I want a particular treatment or not. Consequently, there may be a need for someone to accept or refuse medical intervention for me in consultation with my physicians. I authorize either:

1) Name_____ Phone_____
   Address_____ Relationship_____

Or:

2) Name_____ Phone_____
   Address_____ Relationship_____

as my proxy(s) to make the decision for me whenever my wishes expressed in this document are insufficient or undecided. Should there be any disagreement between the wishes I have indicated in this document and the decisions favored by my above proxy(s) to have authority over any medical directive/ I wish my medical directive to have authority over my proxy(s).

Should there be any disagreement between the wishes of my proxies, the following person shall have final authority.

Name_____ Phone_____
Address_____ Relationship_____

_____   _____
Signature   Address

Signed in the presence of:

_____   _____
Witness   Address
_____   _____
Witness   Address

behalf should a case concerning your health care go to court.

Which to Choose?

How do you decide which is better for you, a living will or a durable power of attorney for health care? Well, it pretty much boils down to that fact that a living will doesn't allow you to name someone to make your medical decisions, so if this is something that you can even remotely imagine being necessary for you, take it into account.

Legalities

Be aware that laws governing Advance Directives differ from state to state. And laws honoring Advance Directives from one state to another aren't always reciprocal. So if you live in one state but must travel to other states frequently, you should probably consider confirming that your Advance Directive passes muster in other jurisdictions. Call your state's Office of the Attorney General (or get your lawyer to do it for a fee).

Canceling an Advance Directive

It's very possible to have a change of heart regarding the details of your Advance Directive. Charlie was sure he'd want his children to do most anything necessary to sustain his life in the event the worst happened. Then he witnessed the drawn-out

SMART SOURCES

Each state offers its own living will documents. All are available free, by downloading to your computer or by request in writing, from Choices in Dying.

Choices in Dying
200 Varick St.
New York, NY 10014
www.choices.org

SMART SOURCES

If you need help preparing an Advance Directive, or you would like more information about them, you may consult your state's Attorney General's Office, the State Office on Aging, or an insurance counseling program for Medicare beneficiaries.

efforts to keep his wife, Faith, alive after she suffered a massive heart attack. After a month of dramatic treatments and surgery, Faith passed on, in great pain and never having recovered enough even to say good-bye to her loved ones. Charlie's idea of what was "necessary" and what was preferable to him changed entirely. And so, then, did his Advance Directive.

You may change or cancel your Advance Directive at any time. Any change or cancellation should be written, signed, and dated. Give copies to your doctor and to anyone else to whom you may have given copies of the original. If you want to change your Advance Directive while you are in the hospital, notify your doctor, family, and lawyer, if possible. Even without a change committed to paper, an oral instruction to your doctor generally carries more weight than a living will or durable power of attorney as long as you can decide and communicate for yourself.

Who Holds a Copy?

You don't have to have an Advance Directive if you don't want one. If you do have an Advance Directive, tell your family about it and make sure they know where it's located. Tell your lawyer about it and tell your doctor about it—and make sure each has a copy in your file. (It's not going to do you or anyone else any good all squirreled away in your sock drawer.) Finally, if you have a durable power of attorney for health care, be sure to give a copy of the original to the person who is named as the attorney.

Choosing Your Representative

Like choosing a personal guardian for your children, the act of deciding to whom you'd like to give a durable power of attorney for health care can prove an emotional decision. Still, if you want to ensure that your medical wishes are carried out when you are no longer capable of expressing them—it's a job that needs to be done.

The issue of a court battle at the end of your life may seem ridiculous, but you may have relatives or other loved ones who simply refuse to accept that it's your time to go. Say you have stated, in a living will, that you do not want the a ventilator employed to keep you breathing when you would otherwise surely die. Your daughter simply may not be able to accept this decision, and challenge your wishes in court. The person holding your durable power of attorney would speak on your behalf.

Consider the following factors in determining who you want to act as your health-care voice.

• **Physical proximity.** Your ultimate health-care crisis may be unforeseen. If you are terminally injured in a car wreck, you want someone who can get to the hospital quickly to see that medical personnel respect your health-care wishes. Therefore, if you live in Oklahoma, you may not want to appoint your closet friend, a Pennsylvania resident, to hold your durable power of attorney.

• **Can the person you choose go along with your wishes?** You may not want surgeons to implant feeding tubes, even if you will no longer be able to eat or drink without them. Can your proxy go

The Choice Is Often Hard for the One Chosen

You met John S. in chapter 3—he was the Florida retiree who gave his son 18 grand to purchase a new pickup.

At 67, he thinks, occasionally, about the end of his life.

"I don't want to be kept alive through any artificial means, period," he says.

He expected his daughter, a believer in one's right to die, to concur with his wishes wholeheartedly.

He brought his living will to her home, expecting her to witness it, and expecting to bestow on her a durable power of attorney for health-care issues.

She reviewed his living will. "I can say no to ventilators," she said. "I can see how he wants no heroic measures made to preserve his life at the end." She couldn't, however, say no to any artificial means needed to feed her father—including the surgical insertion of a feeding tube.

"To me, just letting him starve to death—it seems really, really cruel," she said.

John didn't understand his daughter's hesitation, at first. "She knows these are my wishes. She knows that doctors can pump you with enough pain killers that you feel completely comfortable," he said.

The situation seemed poised to degrade into a war of wills, until John asked his daughter, "Honey, would it be better if I picked someone else?"

She nodded her head vigorously. She was morally unable to accommodate her father's health-care wishes, so John simply picked someone who could.

along with that choice? If he thinks that withholding food and water is cruel, and he's unable to morally support your decision, choose someone else.

• **Backbone.** Your health-care choices may not be the same as wishes your family and friends would have for you. Only give durable power of attorney to those who can lovingly, but firmly, stand up to those who believe that Grandpa should be placed on a respirator because his life should be prolonged at all costs.

Putting the Representation into Effect

You may be choosing to invest a loved one with durable power of attorney for a terminal illness likely not to take place until far into the future. In that case, you should choose a "springing" durable power of attorney—one that takes effect only after certain criteria are met—in this case, an incapacitating illness or accident.

Say, however, you are likely to be incapacitated soon—for example, you have Alzheimer's disease, and you know that your mind is now slowing. Turning over a durable power of attorney outright will allow your designee to be able to speak for you from the moment you sign your living will.

How It Works

Each state offers its own living will document. Get one. Read it to determine which medical help you want when you are in a terminal situation and unable to speak for yourself.

Assign someone your durable power of attorney. You may also want to pick a backup, in case, when the time comes, your first choice is unable to serve.

Sign the document and have it witnessed. Depending on the state in which you live, you may also need to have it notarized. If the stamp of a notary is necessary, your living will form will let you know.

Hand copies of your living will to the person authorized with your durable power of attorney, any physician with whom you closely work, the hospital in which you are likely to be treated, and any close relatives or friends whom you want to know of your choice.

Taking Care of Business

As you face the end of your life, you may need to make some last-minute decisions about your estate. Studying the techniques listed in this book, you've learned how to best provide for your loved ones. Still, you may wonder if there is any way you can minimize a legacy that, despite all your careful planning, has grown too large to escape taxes. You may also fret about who will handle your day-to-day financial affairs as you weaken, and who will handle the bills you've incurred that will come due after your death.

Here are a few suggestions:

• **Give it away now.** You may have thus far hesitated to make charitable bequests or gifts to your loved ones because you wanted to ensure that you would have enough to live on until your dying days. If you health has begun to fail, now may be the time to open your pocketbook. Take advantage of the Unified Estate and Gift Tax credit to give anyone you love a tax-free gift of up to $10,000. This will help minimize your estate, protecting it from a tax levy, and ensure that the money goes to people you love, not the federal government. Also, if you find yourself with extra cash at the end of your life, consider a charitable bequest. Rules for giving are discussed thoroughly in chapter 4.

• **Instruct your heirs to pay any debts from your estate.** Too often, an heir faced with telephone calls from creditors will pay Mom's or Dad's Visa bill from her own pocket, accepting reimbursement from the estate later on.

This is a bad idea. First, as discussed in chapter 2, your heirs bear absolutely no responsibility for your debts. Only your estate needs to pay up. Second, if you are leaving an estate that sits somewhere on the border of exceeding the estate-tax credit cap, your heirs, by paying your bills themselves, may unwittingly enlarge your estate to the point that it's subject to federal taxation.

If you're dying with some debts outstanding—hospital bills, credit card debts, even utility bills—make sure your heirs know that the debts should be paid from estate funds, not their personal pocketbooks.

It works like this: After your death, your executor or trustee will inventory your estate—your assets and debts. He pays your debts from available estate funds before disbursing your assets in accordance with your plan. If you have used a will as your primary estate-planning tool, no debts can be paid off until probate is established. This, as discussed earlier in the book, can take months.

In the meantime, if your heirs are being hassled by creditors, they should tell them that their debtor has died and that they'll get their money as soon as the estate is settled. Some creditors may ask for a copy of the appropriate death certificate, which your heirs should provide to them. They should not, however, cover these debts with their own personal funds.

• **Give someone durable power of attorney for finances.** Above, you learned about durable power attorney for health care and "springing" durable power of attorney for health care. The same legal options hold true for the care of your finances. If you worry that, at some future time, you will be unable to handle your financial concerns, give a trusted friend or relative a "springing" durable power of attorney—one that takes effect only in the event of your incapacitation. If you know that your incapacitation is imminent, offer someone a straight durable power of attorney—one that takes effect the moment you sign the document. Obviously, giving someone else complete control of your financial affairs is a situation fraught with disturbing possibilities. You don't want him spending your money on a trip to Tahiti when you need the cash to pay for medical bills. Talk to a qualified lawyer.

More than Money: Ethical Wills

You've used a "last will and testament" to pass on your assets. You've signed a living will to help ensure that your health-care directives are fulfilled when you are no longer capable of speaking for yourself.

But besides the example you set through the way you lived your life and the manner in which

Information for Benefits Filing and Death Certificate

This sort of detailed information may not be right at the top of your loved ones' minds (or even at their fingertips) when you pass. But it's critical for the filing of a death certificate or for immediate application for death benefits. So get it together and make it handy for those you leave behind. Keep a few copies with all your other pertinent documents in your estate box, file, or drawer.

- Full name:

- Address and phone number:

- Citizenship:

- Race:

- Place of birth:

- Date of birth:

- Social Security number:

- Occupation or type of business:

- Branch of military service:
    Serial number:
    Date and place entered service:
    Date discharged:

- Marital status:

- Spouse's full name:

- Name of next of kin (other than spouse):
    Relationship:
    Address and phone number:

- Father's full name and place of birth:

- Mother's maiden name and place of birth:

SMART SOURCES

Want to know more about ethical wills? Check out the book *So That Your Values Live On: Ethical Wills and How to Prepare Them* coedited by Rabbi Jack Riemer and Nathaniel Stampfer (Jewish Lights Publishing, 1991).

you attempted to raise your children, how do you leave your loved ones your ethics? Your moral code?

Your life has undoubtedly proven more than an accumulation of dollars and cents. An ethical will—a written statement to your loved ones about the moral code you have developed—is your last opportunity to pass on to future generations your beliefs, and whatever knowledge you've gleaned from your time on this earth. Store it with your other estate-planning documents for easy retrieval by your loved ones after your death.

You don't need a lawyer to draw up an ethical will. And, unlike the countless other conversations you've had with your offspring, this time, the kids will listen. Guaranteed.

How to Write an Ethical Will

While you want your heirs to take your ethical will as seriously as any other estate-planning document, it's the easiest one to write. It is in no way legally binding. You don't need any lawyers. You don't need any witnesses. You can write the whole thing during a few hours at your kitchen table, or in front of your computer.

Think about the ethics by which you have tried to live. We forget so much of our day-to-day lives, you may need something to jog your memory. You may want to reread your favorite passages from the Torah, Koran, Bible, or other religious texts. You may turn to a favorite piece of poetry or other literature. Anything that has spoken to your heart can help remind you of the principles you try to practice.

If there is a single rule about writing an ethical

will, it's this: Don't try to control your loved ones from your grave. Don't use your last chance to talk to your friends and relatives as an opportunity to condemn what you view as bad behavior. No one wants her last words from her mother to be, "To my daughter, Mary: I leave you the wish that you would dump your good-for-nothing husband, Harry, and marry someone who can actually hold a job."

Here are some general guidelines to follow when writing your ethical will:

- **Consider the form you want your will to take.** You may want to write a general statement of your beliefs or you may want to "leave" certain people certain moral legacies: "To my beloved son, Matthew, I leave my love of music, with the sincere wish that he'll continue to listen to the Basic Brahms radio program each Sunday. To my daughter, Sarah, I leave my abiding respect for her courage and grace in the face of adversity." You may also want to combine the two forms, starting off with a general statement and moving on to specific legacies.

- **Write a statement of how you tried to live your life.** If you value kindness above all human qualities, say so. If moral courage matters to you, make sure your heirs know. You might also want to include advice on how to overcome life's adversities, how to give something back to the community, how to treat others with respect and love, how to take care for oneself.

- **Avoid the obvious.** If you're writing an ethical will for grown children or other adults, you probably don't need to say, "Don't use drugs. Brush your

Sample Ethical Will

Dear Katie and Zak:

What twist of fate gave your dad the aptitude in math that allowed him to skip a grade and end up sitting next to me in Senior calculus? If Mark were only average bright, he wouldn't have met me, and you wouldn't be here. And then my parents. My mother met my father while she was dating his brother, Tom. If she had ended up with the man who became my uncle, I wouldn't be here, so you wouldn't be here. And if my grandparents . . . Well. You get the gist.

A similar chain of statistically improbable events formed the families that gave birth to all of you—my husband, my children, my friends. God stacked the astral deck against your existences. Still, you're here. Your birth, your life, serves a purpose. I don't know what it is. You probably don't, either. Maybe the purpose isn't for us to see. But it's there.

Be kind. I have always most enjoyed people who are funny and strong and smart and kind. It has lately occurred to me that kindness is the only one of these traits that you can easily develop. I think that our IQs, our senses of humor, and perhaps our emotional stability are largely determined at birth. But anyone can act with kindness, and too few people do—even the strong and smart and funny ones. Forgive everything. Carrying around all the hurts that life can impart will wither your spirit. Seek forgiveness for the hurt you cause. Forget nothing. Every experience—good or bad—changes us, makes us wiser if we learn from it.

Tell the truth, but as gently as possible.

Surround yourself with people who absolutely love you. If someone doesn't absolutely love you, you absolutely don't have the time to continue the relationship. Learn how to love. Don't mistake it for the warm and fuzzy feeling you carry in your heart for another. True love—parental, platonic, or romantic—is a series of actions. Love is listening when you're too bored to listen anymore, and caring when you're too tired to care.

For reasons of their own, some people will hurt you—those who love you, those who don't, those who only pretend to. Good relationships can, and should, weather mistakes. But don't indulge in unhealthy relationships. Wrap your blessing around your friend or lover or spouse like a blanket, and allow him to find his independent way in the world.

Be very, very gentle with others' hearts. You have to treat everybody with God's love and respect. You don't have to like everybody. You don't have to have everybody over to your house for pizza and beer.

Love yourself absolutely.

Avoid anyone who tells you she has dozens of best friends. She doesn't know the meaning of the words. Enjoy your dozens of acquaintances, pals, and buddies, but recognize the difference between these relationships and those you enjoy with your close friends. Close friendship takes as much work as any marriage, and is as rewarding.

Do not tolerate bigotry, or racism, or misogyny, even when it's masked as humor. Fight for the right. If you don't know what "the right" is, pray for guidance. Counter your fear with courage, in any situation—from a lover dumping you to a government gone awry. Remember the words of Robert Browning: "For sudden, the worst turns the best to the brave."

Work hard, but don't fall into the workaholism that plagues this society. Barbara Bush put it best: "No one lies on his deathbed thinking, 'Gee, I wish I'd spent more time at the office.'" Laugh. Rose Kennedy said you should never pass up an opportunity to have fun—you don't know what experience sits around the corner. Never ignore a noble impulse.

Continue watching *It's a Wonderful Life* each Christmas Eve. (Don't forget—you'll find the hot-chocolate recipe stored in my personal cookbook.)

Mark, I leave you with the knowledge that you were the great love of my life. Katie, I leave you my gratitude. A mother can enjoy no greater gift than her daughter growing up to be her best girlfriend. Your kindness and strength have drawn me to you—not from maternal obligations, but from sheer want. Zak, I leave you pure joy. I'm just returning to you what you've given to me.

Remember this: Happiness is the way fresh-brewed coffee smells in the morning, the way a loyal dog will place his head on your knee, the feel of a child's hand reaching out for yours, laughter shared with a spouse or lover, the touch of a friend. Change what you must, but love what you have.

There is a God. Find Him.

Hope is great. Faith is better. I love you.

teeth." You've been saying this for decades. They know, by now.

• **Consider including family traditions.** If your family spent its happiest moments at your home on Christmas Eve, setting up the tree, and re-telling the stories of how each heirloom ornament was passed down, suggest that your heirs carry on this tradition.

It's Your Funeral

Your funeral is the last chance your relatives and friends have to say good-bye to you. It's also your last chance to say good-bye to them. Knowing this, you may want to take an active hand in planning your send-off now, while you're still hale and hearty. Your planning can cover both the financial and sentimental aspects of the event.

Prepaid Funeral Policies

Most large funeral homes today offer a variety of prepaid funeral plans, allowing you to pay, long before you need the services, for your burial plot or crypt, casket, cremation, and viewing room.

Prepaid funeral plans have two distinct advantages over traditional "pay when the person dies" ethic. First, your loved ones will suffer great emotional pain and stress after your death. A prepaid funeral plan helps to lessen that burden. They won't have to go down to the funeral parlor and figure out what casket Dad would have wanted. They won't have to worry about whether they're getting a decently priced plan, or whether a less-than-reputable business person is taking advantage of their grief. They won't have to worry about how to scrape up several thousand dollars in the days immediately following your death. You have removed these burdens from them.

Second, paying now may save your estate cash later. This is why: Prices increase. It's a fact of life. If you buy a prepaid funeral plan now, you're locking into today's rates—and today's rates, as a general rule, will be less expensive than the fees for services charged when you die sometime in the future.

Budget Funeral Help

The cost of a funeral can be ridiculously high. Before you shell out more money than necessary—or make your heirs foot the bill—think a bit about the purpose of the service. Who is it for? Are you trying to impress anyone? If so, why? Maybe there's an emotional reason, such as reassurance, for spending a lot on a luxurious casket. But maybe you're just being swayed by effective sales pressure. The point is to be aware of exactly why you're spending each dollar.

Also, be aware that there are certain funeral benefits many organizations provide. They are often not very well advertised, so you need to take the initiative and check. For example, did you know that if you're a veteran of any of the military forces, you qualify for a minimum of $300 for funeral expenses? That figure can go much higher if your death is related to your military service. Other benefits for veterans, whether wartime or peacetime, are free burial and headstones in any national cemetery for the veteran as well as burial for his or her spouse and children. If there is no space available in a national cemetery, a veteran may be subsidized for up to a certain amount for a plot elsewhere.

If you have any connection to the following, it's definitely worth a call to inquire about financial aid for burial costs:

• automobile club membership

• liability insurance

• trade unions (e.g., teamsters, teachers)

• specific occupations (e.g., shipping industry employees)

• fraternal organizations (e.g., Lions, Elks, Masons)

• state employees benefit

Planning Your Send-Off

Your funeral service may give mourners about an hour to say good-bye to you. What do you want them to remember about you? Consider taking some time to write down instructions for your funeral, including them in your overall estate plan. You may want to address:

• Which clergyman you wish to officiate

• Who you want to serve as your pallbearers

- To which charity you want donations in your name to be made

- What music you would like played

- What scripture/other religious passages you would like read

- What poetry you would like recited

- A final letter to your family and friends that you'd like read at the service

- Whether you would like an open, partially open, or closed coffin

- If you are to be cremated, your wishes regarding ashes and any unique service with them.

See Appendix D, pages 203–7, for a copy of a Funeral or Memorial Service Planner.

Your Obituary

It might sound a bit morbid but, since no one knows your life as intimately as you do, you might want to take an hour or so to write your own obituary.

Different size newspapers allow varying amounts of space for obituaries. In general, the larger the periodical's circulation, the less space they allot for each.

Take a few moments to sit down and write your obituary, including all the accomplishments of your life—your degrees, your jobs, your hobbies, your spouse, children, and grandchildren. You may also want to include instructions to mourners regarding donations to charity to be made in your memory. Larger newspapers will edit your obituary for writing style, content, and space. Smaller paper may run the whole thing verbatim.

If you don't think your regional newspaper will allow you the obituary space you want, consider instructing your heirs to take out a paid "death notice." For a small fee, they'll purchase space in the newspaper—space in which the paper will run your obituary as you wrote it.

Estate-Planning To-Do List

If all you need to do to get your affairs in order could be summed up in a nutshell kind of way, it'd look something like this Estate-Planning To-Do List:

1. Express in writing your wishes regarding the ultimate disposition of your estate.

2. Have an up-to-date will that is in agreement with your personal wishes.

3. Name an executor for your estate. (Children and spouses are not recommended.)

4. Prepare a Letter of Instructions.

5. Designate an appropriate adult guardianship arrangement for yourself such as a living trust or durable power of attorney.

6. Provide for personal and financial guardians for your children and any other dependents.

7. Estimate the size of your taxable estate.

8. Evaluate the impact of estate taxes on the estate and plan accordingly.

9. Review the property ownership designations for all assets with regard to estate planning. Should assets be jointly or singly owned, and so on.

10. Consider the effects of any "order of death" provisions in your estate-planning records and official documents.

11. Prepare a living will.

12. If you own property or assets in more than one state, include the appropriate provisions for this in your estate-planning documents.

13. Consider trusts as part of your estate planning as appropriate.

14. If any of your dependents have special needs, address the issue in your estate planning.

15. If you own your own business, reconcile provisions for disposition of the business with your estate planning.

16. Articulate your personal wishes as far as funeral preparations are concerned.

THE BOTTOM LINE

At the end of your life, your physical and emotional comfort become paramount. Appoint attorneys for health care and finance now, while you're still healthy—those who will carry out your last medical wishes and who will take care of your day-to-day financial dealings when illness does hit—so that you will be free of these types of worries in your last days.

If you decide to write an ethical will, terrific. Give your heirs a general outline of your moral code, but don't trying to control their behavior from your grave.

Take the time to plan your funeral—it's your last send-off, and you have a right to have a say in it. Leave this earth as you came in—unburdened and free.

Appendix A: Last Will and Testament of Elvis A. Presley

I, Elvis A. Presley, a resident and citizen of Shelby County, Tennessee, being of sound mind and disposing memory, do hereby make, publish and declare this instrument to be my last will and testament, hereby revoking any and all wills and codicils by me at any time heretofore made.

Item I. Debts, Expenses and Taxes

I direct my Executor, hereinafter named, to pay all of my matured debts and my funeral expenses, as well as the costs and expenses of the administration of my estate, as soon after my death as practicable. I further direct that all estate, inheritance, transfer and succession taxes which are payable by reason under this will, be paid out of my residuary estate; and I hereby waive on behalf of my estate any right to recover from any person any part of such taxes so paid. My Executor, in his sole discretion, may pay from my domiciliary estate all or any portion of the costs of ancillary administration and similar proceedings in other jurisdictions.

Item II. Instruction Concerning Personal Property: Enjoyment in Specie

I anticipate that included as a part of my property and estate at the time of my death will be tangible personal property of various kinds, characters and values, including trophies and other items accumulated by me during my professional career. I hereby specifically instruct all concerned that my Executor, herein appointed, shall have complete freedom and discretion as to disposal of any and all such property so long as he shall act in good faith and in the best interest of my estate and my beneficiaries, and his discretion so exercised shall not be subject to question by anyone whomsoever.

I hereby expressly authorize my Executor and my Trustee, respectively and successively, to permit any beneficiary of any and all trusts created hereunder to enjoy in specie the use or benefit of any household goods, chattels, or other tangible personal property (exclusive of choses in action, cash, stocks, bonds or other securities) which either my Executor or my Trustees may receive in kind, and my Executor and my Trustees shall not be liable for any consumption, damage, injury to or loss of any tangible property so used, nor shall the beneficiaries of any trusts hereunder or their executors or administrators be liable for any consumption, damage, injury to or loss of any tangible personal property so used.

Item III. Real Estate

If I am the owner of any real estate at the time of my death, I instruct and empower my Executor and my Trustee (as the case may be) to hold such real estate for investment, or to sell same, or any portion thereof, as my Executor or my Trustee (as the case may be) shall in his sole judgment determine to be for the best interest of my estate and the beneficiaries thereof.

Item IV. Residuary Trust

After payment of all debts, expenses and taxes as directed under Item I hereof, I give, devise, and bequeath all the rest, residue, and remainder of my estate, including all lapsed legacies and devices, and any property over which I have a power of appointment, to my Trustee, hereinafter named, in trust for the following purposes:

(a) The Trustee is directed to take, hold, manage, invest and reinvent the corpus of the trust and to collect the income therefrom in accordance with the rights, powers, duties, authority and discretion hereinafter set forth. The Trustee is directed to pay all the expenses, taxes and costs incurred in the management of the trust estate out of the income thereof.

(b) After payment of all expenses, taxes and costs incurred in the management of the expenses, taxes and costs incurred in the management of the trust estate, the Trustee is authorized to accumulate the net income or to pay or apply so much of the net income and such portion of the principal at any time and from time to time for health, education, support, comfortable maintenance and welfare of: (1) My daughter, Lisa Marie Presley, and any other lawful issue I might have, (2) my grandmother, Minnie Mae Presley, (3) my father, Vernon E. Presley, and (4) such other relatives of mine living at the time of my death who in the absolute discretion of my Trustees are in need of emergency assistance for any of the above mentioned purposes and the Trustee is able to make such distribution without affecting the ability of the trust to meet the present needs of the first three numbered categories of beneficiaries herein mentioned or to meet the reasonably expected future needs of the first three classes of beneficiaries herein mentioned. Any decision of the Trustee as to whether or not distribution, to any of the persons described hereunder shall be final and conclusive and not subject to question by any legatee or beneficiary hereunder.

(c) Upon the death of my Father, Vernon E. Presley, the Trustee is instructed to make no further distributions to the fourth category of beneficiaries and such beneficiaries shall cease to have any interest whatsoever in this trust.

(d) Upon the death of both my said father and my said grandmother, the Trustee is directed to divide the Residuary Trust into separate and equal trusts, creating one such equal trust for each of my lawful children then surviving and one such equal trust for the living issue collectively, if any, of any deceased child of mine. The share, if any, for the issue of any such deceased child, shall immediately vest in such issue in equal shares but shall be subject to the provisions of Item V herein. Separate books and records shall be kept for each trust, but it shall not be necessary that a physical division of the assets be made as to each trust.

The Trustee may from time to time distribute the whole or any part of the net income or principal from each of the aforesaid trusts as the Trustee, in its uncontrolled discretion, considers necessary or desirable to provide for the comfortable support, education, maintenance, benefit and general welfare of each of my children. Such distributions may be made directly to such beneficiary or to the guardian of the person of such beneficiary and without responsibility on my Trustee to see to the application of any such distributions, and in making such distributions, the Trustee shall take into account all other sources of funds known by the Trustee to be available for each respective beneficiary for such purpose.

(e) As each of my respective children attains the age of twenty-five (25) years and provided that both my father and my grandmother are deceased, the trust created hereunder for such child care terminates, and all the remainder of the assets then contained in said trust shall be distributed to such child so attaining the age of twenty-five (25) years outright and free of further trust.

(f) If any of my children for whose benefit a trust has been created hereunder should die before attaining the age of twenty-five (25) years, then the trust created for such a child shall terminate on his death, and all remaining assets then contained in said trust shall be distributed outright and free of further trust and in equal shares to the surviving issue of such deceased child but subject to the provisions of Item V herein; but if there be no such surviving issue, then to the brothers and sisters of such deceased child in equal shares, the issue of any other deceased child being entitled collectively to their deceased parent's share. Nevertheless, if any distribution otherwise becomes payable outright and free of trust under the provisions of this paragraph (f) of the Item IV of my will to a beneficiary for whom the Trustee is then administering a trust for the benefit of such beneficiary under provisions of this last will and testament, such distribution shall not be paid outright to such beneficiary but shall be added to and become a part of the trust so being administered for such beneficiary by the Trustee.

Item V. Distribution to Minor Children

If any share of corpus of any trust established under this will become distributable outright and free of trust to any beneficiary before said beneficiary has attained the age of eighteen (18) years, then said share shall immediately vest in said beneficiary, but the Trustee shall retain possession of such share during the period in which such beneficiary is under the age of eighteen (18) years, and, in the meantime, shall use and expend so much of the income and principal for the care, support, and education of such beneficiary, and any income not so expended with respect to each share so retained all the power and discretion had with respect to such trust generally.

Item VI. Alternate Distributees

In the event that all of my descendants should be deceased at any time prior to the time for the termination of the trusts provided for herein, then in such event all of my estate and all the assets of every trust to be created hereunder (as the case may be) shall then distributed outright in equal shares to my heirs at law per stripes.

Item VII. Unenforceable Provisions

If any provisions of this will are unenforceable, the remaining provisions shall, nevertheless, be carried into effect.

Item VIII. Life Insurance

If my estate is the beneficiary of any life insurance on my life at the time of my death, I direct that the proceeds therefrom will be used by my Executor in payment of the debts, expenses and taxes listed in Item I of this will, to the extent deemed advisable by the Executor. All such proceeds not so used are to be used by my Executor for the purpose of satisfying the devises and bequests contained in Item IV herein.

Item IX. Spendthrift Provision

I direct that the interest of any beneficiary in principal or income of any trust created hereunder shall not be subject to claims of creditors or others, nor to legal process, and may not be voluntarily or involuntarily alienated or encumbered except as herein provided. Any bequests contained herein for any female shall be for her sole and separate use, free from the debts, contracts and control of any husband she may ever have.

Item X. Proceeds From Personal Services

All sums paid after my death (either to my estate or to any of the trusts created hereunder) and resulting from personal services rendered by me during my lifetime, including, but not limited to, royalties of all nature, concerts, motion picture contracts, and personal appearances shall be considered to be income, notwithstanding the provisions of estate and trust law to the contrary.

Item XI. Executor and Trustee

I appoint as executor of this, my last will and testament, and as Trustee of every trust required to be created hereunder, my said father.

I hereby direct that my said father shall be entitled by his last will and testament, duly probated, to appoint a successor Executor of my estate, as well as a successor Trustee or successor Trustees of all the trusts to be created under my last will and testament.

If, for any reason, my said father be unable to serve or to continue to serve as Executor and/or as Trustee, or if he be deceased and shall not have appointed a successor Executor or Trustee, by virtue of his last will and testament as stated above, then I appoint National Bank of Commerce, Memphis, Tennessee, or its successor or the institution with which it may merge, as successor Executor and/or as successor Trustee of all trusts required to be established hereunder.

None of the appointees named hereunder, including any appointment made by virtue of the last will and testament of my said father, shall be required to furnish any bond or security for performance of the respective fiduciary duties required hereunder, notwithstanding any rule of law to the contrary.

Item XII. Powers, Duties, Privileges and Immunities of the Trustee

Except as otherwise stated expressly to the contrary herein, I give and grant to the said Trustee (and to the duly appointed successor Trustee when acting as such) the power to do everything he deems advisable with respect to the administration of each trust required to be established under this, my last will and testament, even though such powers would not be authorized or appropriate for the Trustee under statutory or other rules of law. By way of illustration and not in limitation of the generality of the foregoing grant of power and authority of the Trustee, I give and grant to him plenary power as follows:

(a) To exercise all those powers authorized to fiduciaries under the provisions of the Tennessee Code Annotated, Sections 35-616 to 35-618, inclusive, including any amendments thereto in effect at the time of my death, and the same are expressly referred to and incorporated herein by reference.

(b) Plenary power is granted to the Trustee, not only to relieve him from seeking judicial instruction, but to the extent that the Trustee deems it to be prudent, to encourage determinations freely to be made in favor of persons who are the current income beneficiaries. In such instances the rights of all subsequent beneficiaries are subordinate, and the Trustee shall not be answerable to any subsequent beneficiary for anything done or omitted in favor of a current income beneficiary may compel any such favorable or preferential treatment. Without in anywise minimizing or impairing the scope of this declaration of intent, it includes investment policy, exercise of discretionary power to pay or apply principal and income, and determination principal and income questions;

(c) It shall be lawful for the Trustee to apply any sum that is payable to or for the benefit of a minor (or any other person who in the Judgment of the Trustee, is incapable of making proper disposition thereof) by payments in discharge of the costs and expenses of educating, maintaining and supporting said beneficiary, or to make payment to anyone with whom said beneficiary resides or who has the care or custody of the beneficiary, temporarily or permanently, all without intervention of any guardian or like fiduciary. The receipt of anyone to whom payment is so authorized to be made shall be a complete discharge of the Trustee without obligation on his part to see to the further application hereto, and without regard to other resource that the beneficiary may have, or the duty of any other person to support the beneficiary;

(d) In Dealing with the Trustee, no grantee, pledge, vendee, mortgage, lessee or other transference of the trust properties, or any part thereof, shall be bound to inquire with respect to the purpose or necessity of any such disposition or to see to the application of any consideration therefore paid to the Trustee.

Item XIII. Concerning the Trustee and the Executor

(a) If at any time the Trustee shall have reasonable doubt as to his power, authority or duty in the administration of any trust herein created, it shall be lawful for the Trustee to obtain the advice and counsel of reputable legal counsel without resorting to the courts for instructions; and the Trustee shall be fully absolved from all liability and damage or detriment to the various trust estates of any beneficiary thereunder by reason of anything done, suffered or omitted pursuant to advice of said counsel given and obtained in good faith, provided that nothing contained herein shall be construed to prohibit or prevent the Trustee in all proper cases from applying to a court of competent jurisdiction for instructions in the administration of the trust assets in lieu of obtaining advice of counsel.

(b) In managing, investing, and controlling the various trust estates, the Trustee shall exercise the judgment and care under the circumstances then prevailing, which men of prudence, discretion and judgment exercise in the management of their own affairs, not in regard to speculation, but in regard to the permanent disposition of their funds, considering the probable income as well as the probable safety of their capital, and, in addition, the purchasing power of income distribution to beneficiaries.

(c) My Trustee (as well as my Executor) shall be entitled to reasonable and adequate compensation for the fiduciary services rendered by him.

(d) My Executor and his successor Executor and his successor Executor shall have the same rights, privileges, powers and immunities herein granted to my Trustee wherever appropriate.

(e) In referring to any fiduciary hereunder, for purposes of construction, masculine pronouns may include a corporate fiduciary and neutral pronouns may include an individual fiduciary.

Item XIV. Law Against Perpetuities

(a) Having in mind the rule against perpetuities, I direct that (notwithstanding anything contained to the contrary in this last will and testament) each trust created under this will (except such trusts as have heretofore vested in compliance with such rule or law) shall end, unless sooner terminated under other provisions of this will, twenty-one (21) years after the death of the last survivor of such of the beneficiaries hereunder as are living at the time of my death; and thereupon that the property held in trust shall be distributed free of all trust to the persons then entitled to receive the income and/or principal therefrom, in the proportion in which they are then entitled to receive such income.

(b) Notwithstanding anything else contained in this will to the contrary, I direct that if any distribution under this will become payable to a person for whom the Trustee is then administering a trust created hereunder for the benefit of such person, such distribution shall be made to such trust and not to the beneficiary outright, and the funds so passing to such trust shall become a part thereof as corpus and be administered and distributed to the same extent and purpose as if such funds had been a part of such a trust at its inception.

Item XV. Payment of Estate and Inheritance Taxes

Notwithstanding the provisions of Item X herein, I authorize my Executor to use such sums received by my estate after my death and resulting from my personal services as identified in Item X as he deem necessary and advisable in order to pay the taxes referred to in Item I of my said will.

In WITNESS WHEREOF, I, the said ELVIS A. PRESLEY, do hereunto set my hand and seal in the presence of two (2) competent witnesses, and in their presence do publish and declare this instrument to be my Last Will and Testament, this 3 day of March, 1977.

[Signed by Elvis A. Presley]
ELVIS A. PRESLEY

The foregoing instrument, consisting of this and eleven (11) preceding typewritten pages, was signed, sealed, published and declared by ELVIS A. PRESLEY, the Testator, to be his Last Will and Testament, in our presence, and we, at his request and in his presence and in the presence of each other, have hereunto subscribed our names as witnesses, this 3 day of March, 1977, at Memphis, Tennessee.

Witnessed by:

Ginger Alden residing
Charles F. Hodge
Ann Dewey Smith

State of Tennessee
County of Shelby

Appendix B: Sample Draft of a Last Will and Testament

I, _____, currently residing at _____, being of sound and disposing mind, memory, and understanding, do hereby declare the following to be my Last Will and Testament, hereby revoking any and all former Wills and Codicils by me heretofore at any time.

FIRST: I direct that my executor, hereinafter named, pay all of my just debts, funeral expenses, and expense of administration of my estate as soon as may be practicable.

SECOND: I give, devise and bequeath all my right, title, and interest to such real property used by me as a place of residence, which I may own at the time of my death, together with the buildings and improvements thereon and the appurtenances thereto, and all china, silverware, furniture, furnishing, and other articles of household equipment, books, and pictures situated in or about said real property, and all my right, title, and interest in and to any and all policies of insurance relating to such property, subject to all mortgages and liens affecting the same, to my wife _____, absolutely, if she shall survive me.

THIRD: (A) I give and bequeath to my wife _____, absolutely, if she shall survive me, all the rest of my tangible property, including but not limited to personal effects, jewelry, china, silverware, clothing, furniture, furnishings, and other articles of household equipment, books, pictures, and automobiles; but if she shall not survive me, I give, devise, and bequeath said property to my children in as nearly equal shares as possible, as they shall select with the assistance of my Executor, having due regard for their personal preferences, or if only one of them shall survive me, all to the survivor.

(B) I give, devise, and bequeath the rest and residue of my estate (my "residuary estate"), whether real or personal property, tangible or intangible property, wherever located to my wife _____.

FOURTH: If my wife _____ predeceases me, I give, devise, and bequeath the rest and residue of my property which shall be divided in equal shares according to the number of my children surviving me so that there is one trust for each child, to my Trustee, in trust, to hold, manage, invest, and reinvest the same, to collect and receive the income therefrom and until each child for whom a trust is established shall attain the age of twenty-two (22) years of age, to pay or apply the net income therefrom at least semiannually, and to invade the trust and pay or apply so much or all of the principal thereof, to or for the use of each of my children in such amounts and proportions as my Trustee in his discretion shall from time to time determine, or to accumulate same. In paying or applying such principal or income, my Trustee in his discretion shall take into consideration the best interests and welfare of my children. Upon each child then living attaining the age of twenty-two (22) years of age, I give, devise, and bequeath the principal of such trust, or my residuary estate, as the case may be, to such children then living, per stirpes.

FIFTH: Notwithstanding anything herein to the contrary, in the event any beneficiary hereunder and I shall die at the same time, or as a result of a common accident or catastrophe, or under circumstances such as render it difficult or impossible to determine which of us shall have been the first to die, I direct that I shall be deemed to have survived, and that this my Will shall be so construed.

SIXTH: I hereby nominate, constitute, and appoint my wife _____, Executrix of this my Will. In the event she shall predecease me, or shall fail to qualify, or, having qualified, shall die, resign, or cease to act for any reason as Executrix, I hereby nominate, constitute, and appoint my brother and his wife, _____ and _____, residing in _____, to be Co-Executors of this my Will in her place and stead with all the powers and duties herein granted.

I hereby nominate, constitute, and appoint _____, residing at _____, my Trustee of the Trust for my children under Article "Fourth" of this my Last Will and Testament.

I direct that no bond or other security shall be required of any Executor or Trustee herein named for the faithful performance of his duties as Executor or Trustee with respect to the administration of my estate or any trust hereunder, nor with respect to any advance payment of commissions, in any jurisdiction. All the duties and powers, discretionary and otherwise, imposed or conferred upon my Executor an trustee shall devolve upon their successors.

SEVENTH: If my wife _____ shall not survive me, I hereby nominate, constitute, and appoint my brother-in-law and his wife, _____ and _____, presently residing in _____ to be the guardians of the person and property of my minor children surviving me, and I direct that no bond or other security shall be required of any such guardian in any jurisdiction. If _____ and _____ predecease me and my wife, or both die while they are guardians of my minor children, then I hereby nominate, constitute, and appoint my sister-in-law and her husband, _____ and _____, presently residing in _____, as substitute guardians of the person and property of my minor children surviving me.

EIGHTH: In addition to such powers as they may have by law, except as modified by the following powers, I fully authorize and empower my Executor with respect to any and all property, real, personal, or mixed, which may at any time constitute part of my estate, in his sole discretion and without applying to any property at any time held in trust hereunder, whether as principal or income, and until final distribution thereof, in his sole discretion and without applying to any court for permission so to do or for instructions in regard thereto, to retain such property for so long as they may deem advisable, whether or not authorized by law for the investment of trust funds and regardless of any rule as to diversity of trust investments; to borrow money from any person or corporation, including my Executor, and to pledge or mortgage such property as security therefore to employ attorneys, investment counsel, and accountants or other agents and to open and maintain a custodian account and an investment counsel account or accounts and to pay their fees from principal or income; to hold property in the name of a nominee or in such form that title thereto may pass by delivery; to treat as income any and all cash dividends, whether ordinary or extraordinary, except liquidating dividends, warrants, rights, and similar incidents of stock ownership; to carry out any direction or authorization to pay over income or principal to any beneficiary by applying the same for the benefit of such beneficiary; and, generally, to do all such acts and take all such proceedings with respect to such property as if the absolute owner thereof, and no person dealing with my said Executor shall be obligated to see to the proper applications of any monies paid or delivered.

IN WITNESS WHEREOF, I have hereunto signed my name and affixed my seal to this my Last Will and Testament this _____ day of ____, in the Year Two Thousand.

Appendix C:
What to Include in a Letter of Instructions

Anticipated Benefits
(Sources and Amounts)

- Employer:
    - **a.** Contact:
    - **b.** Address:
    - **c.** Phone:

- Life insurance $_____
- Pension $_____
- Profit sharing $_____
- Accident insurance $_____
- Other $_____

- Insurance $_____
- Social Security $_____
- Veterans Administration $_____
- Other $_____

Contact Names and Numbers

- Employer
- Funeral home
- Lawyer
- Newspapers (for obituary information)
- Social Security office
- Bank (regarding mortgage)
- Insurance companies
- Accountant or financial planner

- Close relatives
- Acquaintances and organizations

Information for the Funeral Director

- Complete name
- Address
- Marital status and name of spouse
- Birth date and place of birth
- Father's name and place of birth
- Mother's name and place of birth
- Military record
- Social Security number
- Occupation
- Life insurance policy or policies (if proceeds cover funeral expenses)
- Request for copies of the death certificate (you may need as many as ten)
- Any special requests or provisions

Cemetery

- Location
- Date purchased
- Deed number
- Location of deed
- Perpetual care (Y/N)

Locations of Key Documents

- Will
- Power of attorney
- Living will
- Letter of instructions
- Birth certificate

- Baptismal, communion, confirmation papers
- Diplomas
- Marriage certificate
- Military records
- Immigration or naturalization records
- Adoption papers
- Divorce records
- List of financial assets
- Memberships
- Subscriptions
- Passport

Income Tax Returns

- Location of all previous federal, state, and local returns
- Accountant or preparer's name and phone number
- Location of estimated tax file. Make note to check to see if estimated taxes are due.

Physicians

- Doctor's name, address, phone
- Dentist's name, address, phone
- Children's pediatrician's name, address, phone
- Children's dentist's name, address, phone
- Spouse's doctor's name, address, phone
- Spouse's dentist's name, address, phone

Banking

- Checking account:
  a. Bank name and address
  b. Name(s) on account

    c. Account number and type of account
    d. Location of passbook
- Savings account:
    a. Bank name and address
    b. Name(s) on account
    c. Account number and type of account
    d. Location of passbook
- Other account:
    a. Bank name and address
    b. Name(s) on account
    c. Account number and type of account
    d. Location of passbook

Credit Cards
(Include the following information for each card.)

- Company, telephone, address
- Name on card
- Number on card
- Location of card

Loans
(Include the following information for each loan.)

- Bank name and address
- Name on loan
- Account number
- Monthly payment
- Location of papers and payment stubs (if any)
- Is there life insurance on the loan?

Investments
- Stocks
    a. Company

    b. Name on certificate
    c. Number of shares
    d. Purchase price and date
    e. Location of certificate and certificate number(s)

- Bonds
    a. Issuer
    b. Issued to
    c. Face amount
    d. Number of bond
    e. Purchase price and date
    f. Maturity date
    g. Location of certificate

- Mutual Funds
    a. Company
    b. Name on account
    c. Number of shares or units
    d. Location of statements, certificates

- Other

List all other investments, including the amount invested, to whom issued, issuer, maturity date, and other information, along with the location of certificates and documentation.

Debts Owed the Estate

- Name of debtor
- Description
- Terms
- Balance
- Location of documents

Life Insurance

A copy of the death certificate must be sent to each insurance company before you may collect benefits.

- Policy number and amount
- Location of policy
- Name of insured person
- Insurer's name and address
- Type of policy
- Beneficiaries
- Issue date
- Maturity date
- Payout
- Other payout options
- For veterans insurance, give local Veteran's Administration Office phone number.

Homeowners/Renters/Automobile Insurance

- Coverage
- Insurer's name and address
- Policy number
- Location of policy
- Term
- Agent

Medical Insurance

- Coverage
- Insurer's name and address
- Policy number
- Location of policy
- Name and telephone number of employer or other group
- Agent

House, Condo, or Co-Op Information

• Name of contract holder
• Address
• Lot
• Other descriptions as necessary
• Attorney: name and address
• Location of statement of closing, policy of title insurance, deed, land survey, and so on
• Mortgage
  a. Lender
  b. Amount of original mortgage
  c. Date taken out
  d. Amount owed now
  e. Payment method
  f. Location of payment stubs or statements
  g. If there is life insurance on the mortgage, what is the policy number? Location of policy? Annual amount?
• Taxes
  a. Amount
  b. Location of receipts
• Cost of house
  a. Buying price
  b. Closing fees
  c. Other costs associated with purchase
  d. Improvements total $

• List of house improvements, dates, costs, location of bills and receipts
• Location of renter's lease, if any

Contents of the Home
(Ownership of specific items, such as jewelry, musical instruments, computer equipment, appliances, and so on.)

- Name of owners
- Form of ownership
- Location of documents
- Location of inventory
- Location of appraisals
- Location of important warranties, receipts, documents, and so on

Automobiles
(Titles held in the name of the deceased must be changed.)

- Year, make, model
- Body type
- Cylinders
- Color
- Identification number
- Title in name(s) of
- Location of papers (title, registration)

Appendix D: Funeral or Memorial Service Planner

This form does triple duty: it can help you to think about what sort of arrangements you'd like for your own service; it helps your heirs carry out your wishes with a minimum of energy spent on second-guessing; and it helps you to plan a funeral for a loved one.

The Basic Service

- Religious within a specific denomination
- Religious but nondenominational
- Nonreligious
- Funeral with an open casket
- Funeral with a closed casket
- Memorial service with no casket
- Other type of service
- Family only
- Family and most immediate circle of friends
- Open

Logistics

Service or church location:

_____

Contact information for location:

Person_____

Telephone_____

Time and date of service

_____

If there will be visiting hours before the service:

Where_____

When_____

If there is a reception after the service:

Where_____

When_____

Service Program

Type of Music:
- Organ
- Piano
- Violin
- Flute
- Vocal soloist
- Hymns for congregation to sing

Musical Selections:

_____

_____

_____

_____

Musicians:

_____

_____

_____

_____

Readings from sacred texts:

_____

_____

_____

_____

Person or persons officiating:

_____

_____

_____

_____

Eulogies or other personal remembrances:

_____

_____

_____

Speakers:

_____

_____

_____

_____

Poems or other readings:

_____

_____

_____

_____

Readers/performers:

_____

_____

_____

_____

Ritual Elements

- Candle lighting

- Photographs

- Prayers

- Special seating arrangements

- Other

Pallbearers/ushers:

_____

_____

_____

_____

Details
- Program printing
- Refreshments
- Flowers
- Transportation
- Other

Additional Information

_____

_____

_____

_____

Index

stocks, bonds, money
market accounts, and
mutual funds, 21, 198-99
"What I Own" worksheet
and, 33
Property control trusts,
138-39
Property guardians, 127,
131, 132-34
conflicts between personal
guardian and, 133-34
and conflicts of interest
between siblings, 138
for family members with
special needs, 138-40
and trusts to provide for
your children, 135, 136,
138
Property insurance, 10
Prudential, 112
Puerto Rico, 57, 58

Qualified terminable interest (QTIP) trusts, 99
Real estate, 19-20
appraisals of, 10, 20
deeds to, 9, 10
defined, 21
determining worth of, 23
information on, in letter of
instructions, 201
selling to pay estate tax,
5-6
see also Homes
Real property, defined, 21
Registered financial
consultants (RFCs), 39
Relatives, as trustees,
100-101
Religious heritage, guardian
choice and, 128
Renters insurance, 200
Residuary estate, defined,
65
Resources, 4, 5, 6
for advance directives, 155
for appraisers, 22
do-it-yourself will kits, 74
for ethical wills, 164
for family businesses, 142
for life insurance, 110

for professional advisors,
35, 99
for Social Security, 118
for tax information, 53, 55,
56, 88, 95
Retirement plans, 10, 70
Revocable trusts, 85-86
defined, 85
Rhine, David S., 66, 89
Rhode Island, 26, 28, 58, 134
Riemer, Rabbi Jack, 164
*Right Way and the Wrong Way
of Leaving Money to Your
Children (and Others), The*
(G. M. Condon and J. L.
Condon), 142
Royalties, 24

Safety deposit boxes, 9, 12-13
Sentimental value, items
with, 18, 46
Siblings:
conflicts of interest
between, 138
equality of bequests to, 43-
44, 45-46
Sinatra, Barbara Marx, 79
Sinatra, Frank, 79
Small businesses:
estate taxes on, 61
family businesses, 126, 142-
45
life insurance for partners
in, 108
Social Security, 118
disability payments from,
139-40
Sole ownership, 18, 29
*So That Your Values Live On:
Ethical Wills and How to
Prepare Them* (Riemer and
Stampfer), 164
South Carolina, 26, 58, 134,
135
South Dakota, 26, 58, 59,
134
Special needs trusts, 139,
140
Spouse:
A/B trusts and, 84, 86-89
equalizing estate of, 60-62

estate in red and, 32
estate planning with, 25
general power of appoint-
ment trust for, 98-99
gifts to, 57
marital deduction and, 52,
59-60, 88
owning property with, 28-
29
qualified terminable
interest (QTIP) trust for,
99
Social Security benefits
for, 118
state intestacy laws and, 68
trustee choice and, 100
"Springing" durable power
of attorney, 159, 162
Stampfer, Nathaniel, 164
State taxes, 53-54
death, 52, 57, 58
inheritance, 52, 57-59
Stocks, 9, 21
gifts of, 56-57
Storing documents, 9, 12-13,
49-50
advance directives, 156
Succession plans, for family
businesses, 126, 143-45
Supplemental security
income (SSI), 139-40
Supreme Court, U.S., 153
Survivorship life, 114

"Tag" party for heirs, 46
Tanner, John, 61
Taxes, 2, 52-66
death, 52, 57, 58, 63
foreign, 63
income, 10, 52, 197
inheritance, 52, 57-59
legal loopholes and, 59-64
state, 52, 53-54, 57-59
see also Unified Gift and
Estate Tax
Tax preparers, enrolled
agents (EAs) as, 39
Tax returns:
in estate files, 9, 10
letter of instructions and,
197

Books in the
Smart Guide™ series

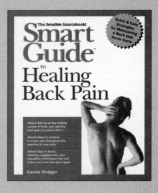
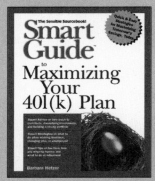

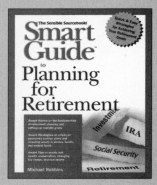
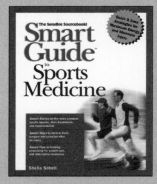
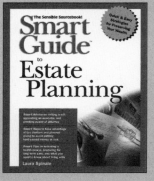

Smart Guide™ to
Estate Planning

Smart Guide™ to
Healing Back Pain

Smart Guide™ to
Maximizing Your
401(k) Plan

Smart Guide™ to
Planning for Retirement

Smart Guide™ to
Sports Medicine

Smart Guide™ to
Yoga

Smart Guide™ to
Boosting Your Energy

Smart Guide™ to
Buying a Home

Smart Guide™ to
Getting Strong and Fit

Smart Guide™ to
Getting Thin and
Healthy

Smart Guide™ to
Healing Foods

Smart Guide™ to
Making Wise
Investments

Smart Guide™ to
Managing Personal
Finance

Smart Guide™ to
Managing Your Time

Smart Guide™ to
Profiting from Mutual
Funds

Smart Guide™ to
Relieving Stress

Smart Guide™ to
Starting a Small Business

Smart Guide™ to
Vitamins and Healing
Supplements